5 · 6

GH00601872

Microsoft Excel 2000
explained

Books Available

By both authors:

BP327 DOS one step at a time
BP337 A Concise User's Guide to Lotus 1-2-3 for Windows
BP341 MS-DOS explained
BP346 Programming in Visual Basic for Windows
BP352 Excel 5 explained
BP362 Access one step at a time
BP387 Windows one step at a time
BP388 Why not personalise your PC
BP400 Windows 95 explained
BP406 MS Word 95 explained
BP407 Excel 95 explained
BP408 Access 95 one step at a time
BP409 MS Office 95 one step at a time
BP415 Using Netscape on the Internet*
BP420 E-mail on the Internet*
BP426 MS-Office 97 explained
BP428 MS-Word 97 explained
BP429 MS-Excel 97 explained
BP430 MS-Access 97 one step at a time
BP433 Your own Web site on the Internet
BP448 Lotus SmartSuite 97 explained
BP456 Windows 98 explained*
BP460 Using Microsoft Explorer 4 on the Internet*
BP464 E-mail and news with Outlook Express*
BP465 Lotus SmartSuite Millennium explained
BP471 Microsoft Office 2000 explained
BP472 Microsoft Word 2000 explained
BP473 Microsoft Excel 2000 explained
BP474 Microsoft Access 2000 explained
BP478 Microsoft Works 2000 explained

By Noel Kantaris:

BP258 Learning to Program in C
BP259 A Concise Introduction to UNIX*
BP284 Programming in QuickBASIC
BP325 A Concise User's Guide to Windows 3.1

Microsoft Excel 2000 explained

by

N. Kantaris
and
P.R.M. Oliver

Bernard Babani (publishing) Ltd
The Grampians
Shepherds Bush Road
London W6 7NF
England

Please Note

Although every care has been taken with the production of this book to ensure that any projects, designs, modifications and/or programs, etc., contained herewith, operate in a correct and safe manner and also that any components specified are normally available in Great Britain, the Publishers and Author(s) do not accept responsibility in any way for the failure (including fault in design) of any project, design, modification or program to work correctly or to cause damage to any equipment that it may be connected to or used in conjunction with, or in respect of any other damage or injury that may be so caused, nor do the Publishers accept responsibility in any way for the failure to obtain specified components.

Notice is also given that if equipment that is still under warranty is modified in any way or used or connected with home-built equipment then that warranty may be void.

British Library Cataloguing in Publication Data:

A catalogue record for this book is available from the British Library

ISBN 0 85934 473 8

Cover Design by Gregor Arthur
Printed and Bound in Great Britain by Bath Press

About this Book

Microsoft Excel 2000 explained has been written for those who want to get to grips with the latest 3-dimensional spreadsheet for Windows 95/98 or higher from Microsoft, in the fastest possible time. The material in this book is presented on the 'what you need to know first, appears first' basis, although the underlying structure is such that slightly more experienced users need not start at the beginning and go right through to the end; they can start from any section, as each section of the book has been designed to be self contained.

No previous knowledge of spreadsheets is assumed, so that users without any knowledge of the subject can follow the book easily, but we do not describe how to set up your computer hardware, or how to install and use Windows. If you need to know more about the Windows environment, then may we suggest you select an appropriate level book for your needs from the 'Books Available' list - the books are graduated in complexity with the less demanding *One step at a time* series, to the more detailed *Explained* series. They are all published by BERNARD BABANI (publishing) Ltd.

Microsoft Excel 2000 is a very powerful spreadsheet package that has the ability to work 3-dimensionally with both multiple worksheets and files. It is operated by selecting commands from drop-down menus, by using buttons, or by writing 'macros' to chain together menu commands. Each method of accessing the package is discussed separately, but the emphasis is mostly in the area of menu-driven and button clicking command selection. Working under the Windows 95/98 or higher environment, gives the package an excellent WYSIWYG (What You See Is What You Get) appearance which, in turn, allows for the production of highly professional quality printed material.

Most features of the package are discussed using simple examples that the user is encouraged to type in, save, and modify as more advanced features are introduced. This provides the new user with a set of examples that aim to help with the learning process, and should help to provide the confidence needed to tackle some of the more advanced capabilities of the package later.

For those who would like to practise with additional examples, slightly unguided, but with enough instruction so that they can be completed successfully, we have included three exercises in Chapter 11. The exercises are drawn from sufficiently general topics, so as to maximise their suitability to your needs and understanding.

Although the book is intended as a supplement to the 'Help' documentation that comes with the package, in the last chapter of the book, all the Excel 2000 functions are listed so that it is self contained and can be used as a reference long after you become an expert in the use of the program.

Microsoft Excel 2000 is an exciting package that will help you with the new millennium challenges and opportunities to business. It offers new tools that use Web technology to provide enhanced workgroup productivity and the ability to access and publish information on the Internet.

This book introduces Excel with sufficient detail to get you working, then discusses how to share information with other people. The book was written with the busy person in mind. It is not necessary to learn all there is to know about a subject, when reading a few selected pages can usually do the same thing quite adequately. With the help of this book, it is hoped that you will be able to come to terms with Microsoft Excel and get the most out of your computer in terms of efficiency, productivity and enjoyment, and that you will be able to do it in the shortest, most effective and informative way.

If you would like to purchase a Companion Disc for any of the listed books by the same author(s), apart from the ones marked with an asterisk, containing the file/program listings which appear in them, then fill in the form at the back of the book and send it to Phil Oliver at the stipulated address.

About the Authors

Noel Kantaris graduated in Electrical Engineering at Bristol University and after spending three years in the Electronics Industry in London, took up a Tutorship in Physics at the University of Queensland. Research interests in Ionospheric Physics, led to the degrees of M.E. in Electronics and Ph.D. in Physics. On return to the UK, he took up a Post-Doctoral Research Fellowship in Radio Physics at the University of Leicester, and then in 1973 a lecturing position in Engineering at the Camborne School of Mines, Cornwall, (part of Exeter University), where between 1978 and 1997 he was also the CSM Computing Manager. At present he is IT Director of FFC Ltd.

Phil Oliver graduated in Mining Engineering at Camborne School of Mines in 1967 and since then has specialised in most aspects of surface mining technology, with a particular emphasis on computer related techniques. He has worked in Guyana, Canada, several Middle Eastern and Asian countries, South Africa and the United Kingdom, on such diverse projects as: the planning and management of bauxite, iron, gold and coal mines; rock excavation contracting in the UK; international mining equipment sales and international mine consulting. In 1988 he took up a lecturing position at Camborne School of Mines (part of Exeter University) in Surface Mining and Management. He retired from full-time lecturing in 1998, to spend more time writing, consulting and developing Web sites for clients.

Acknowledgements

We would like to thank the staff of Microsoft UK and August.one Communications Ltd., for providing the software programs on which this work was based. We would also like to thank colleagues at the Camborne School of Mines for the helpful tips and suggestions which assisted us in the writing of this book.

Trademarks

Arial and **Times New Roman** are registered trademarks of The Monotype Corporation plc.

HP and LaserJet are registered trademarks of Hewlett Packard Corporation.

IBM is a registered trademark of International Business Machines, Inc.

Intel is a registered trademark of Intel Corporation.

Lotus, 1-2-3 are registered trademarks of Lotus Development Corporation, a subsidiary of IBM.

Microsoft, **MS-DOS**, **Windows**, **Windows NT, Works**, and **Visual Basic**, are either registered trademarks or trademarks of Microsoft Corporation.

PostScript is a registered trademark of Adobe Systems Incorporated.

TrueType is a registered trademark of Apple Corporation.

All other brand and product names used in the book are recognised as trademarks, or registered trademarks, of their respective companies.

Contents

1

Package Overview

Microsoft's Excel 2000 for Windows 95/98, or higher, is a powerful and versatile software package which has proved its usefulness, not only in the business world, but also within the scientific and engineering spheres. The program's power lies in its ability to emulate everything that can be done by the use of pencil, paper and a calculator. It is an 'electronic spreadsheet' or simply a 'spreadsheet', and its power is derived from the power of the computer it is running on, and the flexibility and accuracy with which it can deal with the solution of the various applications it is programmed to manage. These can vary from budgeting and forecasting to the solution of complex scientific and engineering problems.

Microsoft Excel 2000 is backwards compatible to spreadsheets built up on previous versions of Excel or, indeed, to other spreadsheets, such as Lotus 1-2-3, Quattro Pro, and Microsoft Works, which can easily be made to run on this version of Excel. Once you have overcome the first hurdle and started to use Excel 2000, you will find it both intuitive and an easy program to produce the type of work output you would not have dreamt possible.

Excel 2000, in common with all other Microsoft Office 2000 applications, makes use of what is known as IntelliSense, which anticipates what you want to do and produces the correct result. For example, AutoCorrect and AutoFormat can, when active, correct common spelling mistakes and format an entire workbook automatically. Other Wizards can help you with everyday tasks and/or make complex tasks easier to manage.

Excel uses Object Linking and Embedding (OLE) to move and share information seamlessly between Office 2000 applications. For example, you can drag information from one application to another, or you can link information from one application into another. Similarly, Hyperlinks can be used from any of the Office 2000 applications to access other Office documents, files on an internal or external Web or FTP (File Transfer Protocol) site, or HTML (Hypertext Markup Language) files. Hyperlinks help you use your documents with the Internet.

Finally, writing macros in Visual Basic gives you a powerful development platform with which to create custom solutions.

Hardware and Software Requirements

If Microsoft Excel 2000 is already installed on your computer, you can safely skip this and the following section of this chapter.

To install and use Excel 2000, which comes as part of Microsoft Office 2000, you need an IBM-compatible PC equipped with Intel's pentium processor. Microsoft suggests a 75 MHz processor for the installation of the Standard edition of Office 2000 which includes Outlook, Word, Excel, and PowerPoint. In addition, you need the following:

- Windows 95/98 (or higher), or Windows NT as the operating system.

- Random access memory (RAM) required is:

- For Windows 9x or higher, 16 MB plus 4 MB for each running application.

- For Windows NT, 32 MB plus 4 MB for each running application.

- Hard disc space required for the Standard edition of Office 2000 is 189 MB.

- CD-ROM drive.

- Video adapter: VGA or higher resolution. If you are embedding colour pictures, you will need a 256-colour video adapter.

- Pointing device: Microsoft Mouse or compatible.

Realistically, to run the above mentioned Office 2000 applications, including Excel 2000, with reasonably sized documents, you will need a 100 MHz Pentium PC with at least 32 MB of RAM. To run Microsoft Office 2000 from a network, you must also have a network compatible with your Windows operating environment, such as Microsoft's Windows 95/98 or higher, Windows NT, LAN Manager, Novell's NetWare, etc.

Finally, if you are connected to the Internet, you can take advantage of Excel's advanced capabilities with the Internet.

Installing Microsoft Office 2000

Installing Office 2000 on your computer's hard disc is made very easy using the SETUP program, which even configures it automatically to take advantage of the computer's hardware. One of SETUP's functions is to convert compressed Office files from the CD-ROM, prior to copying them onto your hard disc.

Note: If you are using a virus detection utility, disable it before running SETUP, as it might conflict with it.

To install Microsoft Office, place the distribution CD in your CD drive and close it. The auto-start program on the CD will start the SETUP program automatically. If that does not work, click the **Start** button, and select the **Run** command which opens the Run dialogue box, shown below.

Next, type in the **Open** box:

```
G:\setup
```

as shown here.

In our case we used the CD-ROM in the G: drive; yours could be different. Clicking the **OK** button, starts the

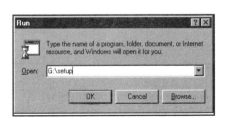

installation of Microsoft Office 2000. SETUP displays the first of several screens.

We suggest that you follow the instructions displayed on the screen. SETUP goes through the following procedure:

- Prompts you to type your name and the name of your organisation (optional).

- Prompts you to type in the Product Key.

- Asks you to accept the licence agreement.

- Prompts you to supply the path to the directory where you want to install Excel, and then checks your system and the available hard disc space.

- Searches your system's discs for other installed Office components and asks you whether an older version of Excel should be removed or not.

Follow the SETUP instructions on the screen, until the installation of Microsoft Office program files is completed. The SETUP program will modify your system files automatically so that you can start Excel easily by creating and displaying a new entry in the **Start, Programs** cascade menu. During installation, if you use the Office Shortcut Bar it is collated and added to the Windows Start Up program so that it will be displayed automatically on your screen whenever you start your PC.

 In addition, Office 2000 adds to the **Start** menu the two entries shown at the top of the adjacent screen dump; the **New Office Document**, and the **Open Office Document**. The first allows you to select in a displayed dialogue box the tab containing the type of document you want to work with, such as letters & faxes, memos, or presentations, to mention but a few. Double-clicking the type of document or template you want, automatically loads the appropriate application. The second entry allows you to work with existing documents. Opening a document, first starts the application originally used to create it, then opens the document.

Adding or Removing Office Applications

To add or remove an Office application at any time, left-click the **Start** button at the bottom left corner of the screen, point to **Settings**, then click the **Control Panel** option on the Windows pop-up menu, as shown below.

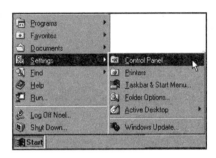

This opens the Control Panel dialogue box. Next, double-click the Add/Remove Programs icon,  shown here to the left, to open the dialogue box below. Click the Install/Uninstall tab and select the Microsoft Office 2000 program, and then click the **Add/Remove** button.

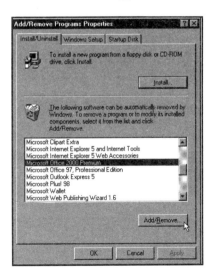

This requires you insert the Office 2000 CD into your CD drive, which causes SETUP to display the following Maintenance Mode dialogue box:

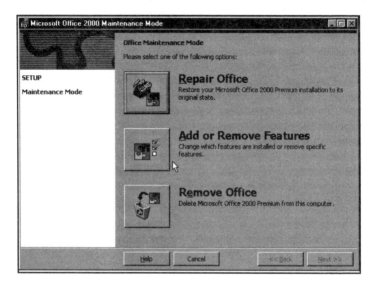

Selecting **Add or Remove Features** opens up the dialogue box to the left in which you can select which Office applications and features you want installed.

Note the additional buttons on the above screen. Use the **Repair Office** button to reinstall the whole of Office 2000, or to find and fix any errors in your original installation. Finally, you can use the **Remove Office** button to uninstall all of the Office 2000 applications.

Major Excel Features

Some of the major features Microsoft Excel 2000 contains, include the ability to:

- Employ the Office Assistant which uses IntelliSense natural-language technology. It anticipates the kind of help you need and suggests Help topics appropriate to the work you are doing at the time. Further, you can have the Assistant offer to start a Wizard when you start certain tasks, such as creating a chart.

- Manage your files from within the Open dialogue box. Right-clicking a workbook opens a shortcut menu, shown here, to help you with appropriate house-keeping functions.

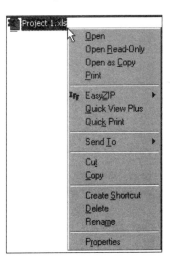

- Enter and edit data directly in a cell or in the formula bar, and to check your spelling.

- Use up to 32,000 characters in a cell.

- Use up to 65,536 rows per worksheet.

- Manage data simply by treating all files as workbooks.

- Open or find documents by clicking the **Open** option on the **File** menu.

- Use the Find File command to search for a workbook, even if its name is not known.

- Use the 'Yes to All' option when closing multiple files.

- Use the Format Painter button to quickly copy formats between cells and between objects.

- Rotate text in cells to any angle, which lets you produce vertical labels.

- Create named ranges in the Name box on the formula bar.

- Create custom AutoFill series and automatically create grand totals with AutoSum.

- Use the AutoCalculate facility which produces the sum of a selected range automatically and displays it on the Status bar at the bottom of the screen.

- Use the AutoComplete facility which allows you to type the first few letters of an entry in a cell, then use the right-mouse button to complete the entry from a list, based on the entries you have already made in that column.

- Use the AutoCorrect facility which when selected, can correct common mistakes as you type.

- Recommend worksheet functions by typing a brief description of what you want to do. The Office Assistant then suggests which worksheet functions to use.

- Use the Chart Wizard, which is integrated with the tabbed dialogue boxes and options, to format and edit your charts.

- Create 3-D formulae and 3-D names for powerful workbook models.

- Drag data directly onto a chart to add a data series or data points, and add trendlines and error bars to your data series.

- Draw graphic objects directly on charts and to position objects, such as titles, anywhere you want them.

- Share the Drawing tools with other Office 2000 applications.

- Use the Graphics Interchange Format (.gif) and JPEG File Interchange Format (.jpg) filters to export charts in common graphics formats so they can be displayed on the World Wide Web.

- Use the drag-and-drop editing facility to easily move or copy selected ranges between worksheets and workbooks.

- Easily locate the row and column headings that apply to the active cell - as you highlight a cell, the row number and column letter 'light up'.

- Sort data by using column labels from a list and the creation of custom sort orders, such as High, Med, and Low.

- Access external databases with Microsoft Query and the use of the interactive PivotTable facility to cross-tabulate and summarise data from an existing list or table.

- Use Queries which now run in the background, so that you can continue to work in Excel while data is being retrieved.

- Use the Scenario Manager to create, manage, and track changes to scenarios.

- Use or customise any of the built-in toolbars, or create your own.

- Use autotemplates to create new default workbooks and sheets.

- Display the precedent, dependent, and error tracers directly on your worksheet to locate problems in formulae.

- Use the Object Linking and Embedding (OLE) facility to link objects without leaving Microsoft Excel.

- Solve What-if problems by seeking a value that solves a formula.

- Use the Solver to analyse multiple-variable problems.

- Use the Data Analysis Tool to make statistical or engineering analysis easier.

- Add explanatory information, called cell tips, to individual worksheet cells.

- Analyse sales or market research data by geographical regions by arranging your data in columns on a worksheet.

- Create shared lists so that several users can work with the same data.

- Use multiple Undo - for up to the last 16 actions.

- Use row and column labels in formulae to refer to cells without using cell references or creating names.

- Use the Visual Basic Programming language to create custom solutions in Microsoft Excel.

- Add menus to toolbars or toolbar buttons to menus. The image associated with a menu command shows you what the command will look like if you choose to display it as a button.

- Use the IntelliMouse pointing device - a mouse introduced with the previous Office release. You can use the wheel button of this mouse to scroll or zoom your view of a worksheet and drill up and down on data in PivotTables, outlines, and subtotalled lists.

Obviously, the list of enhancements does not end here. Other features deal with formatting numbers, charts, organising data, and retrieving and analysing data from lists and tables.

New Features in Excel 2000

Some of the major enhancements Microsoft Excel 2000 has over previous releases of the package allow you to:

- Use the new Office Clipboard to collect objects from all of your programs, including your Web browser, and then paste them when you need them. You can store up to 12 objects on the Office Clipboard.

- Use additional number formats, including the euro currency symbol and four-digit dates.

- Select cells with coloured text, which then remains the same colour instead of appearing in an inverse colour scheme.

- Enter, display, and edit text in all supported languages in any language version of Office 2000.

- Automatically extend formatting and formulas in lists, simplifying this common task.

- Use the new PivotChart report which brings the power of PivotTable reports to your charts. PivotChart reports are interactive, with field buttons that you can use to show and hide items in a chart.

- Make the axis text in charts employing large numbers shorter and more readable by changing the display unit of the axis. For example, if the chart values range from 1,000 to 100,000, you can display the numbers as 1 to 100 on the axis and display a label indicating that the axis units are in thousands.

- Create and run queries to retrieve data available on the Web. You can either select an entire Web page or specify a table on a Web page to retrieve. Excel 2000 provides several sample Web queries that you can run.

- Seamlessly move Excel data to a Web server as interactive spreadsheets and charts.

- Choose where graphics and other supporting files are stored, and specify what format graphics are saved in for use on Web pages.

- Use the Web Folders feature to manage files that you store on a Web server and to put Excel data on the Web. You can access Web Folders through the Windows Explorer, and then use its features to create folders, view properties, and drag-and-drop files on any Web server that you have permissions to do so.

- Use the field drop-down arrows to display and select from a list of available items. The list provides a quick way to show and hide items in fields.

- Make a PivotTable report available on a Web page as a PivotTable list, which is a component that lets users interact with the data in the Web browser. Users can also refresh the data, change the layout, and select different items for display.

- Sign your Visual Basic for Applications macros to identify who authored them and ensure that they are virus-free. Microsoft Excel 2000 recognises signed macros from trusted sources and does not display a warning message unless the macro has been modified in some way.

- Use the Office Assistant out of its box which uses less space on your screen. If the Assistant cannot answer your question, you can ask it to take you to the Web for more information. If you do not like the Assistant, you can turn it off permanently and use the Help index.

Most features of the package (old and new) will be discussed using simple examples that the user is encouraged to type in, save, and modify as more advanced features are introduced. This provides the new user with a set of examples that aim to help with the learning of the most commonly used features of the package, and should help to provide the confidence needed to tackle some of the more advanced features of the package later.

The Mouse Pointers

In Microsoft Excel, as with all other graphical based programs, using a mouse makes many operations both easier and more fun to carry out.

Excel makes use of the mouse pointers available in Windows, some of the most common of which are illustrated below. When Excel is initially started up the first you will see is the hourglass, which turns into either an upward pointing hollow arrow or a hollow depending on the area you point to. Other shapes depend on the type of work you are doing at the time.

 The hourglass which displays when you are waiting while performing a function.

 The arrow which appears when the pointer is placed over menus, scrolling bars, and buttons.

 The hollow cross which appears when the pointer is placed within the worksheet area.

 The I-beam which appears in normal text areas of the screen.

 The 4-headed arrow which appears after choosing the **Control, Move/Size** command(s) for moving or sizing windows.

 The double arrows which appear when over the border of a window, used to drag the side and alter the size of the window.

 The Help hand which appears in the Help windows, and is used to access 'hypertext' type links.

Excel 2000, like other Windows packages, has additional mouse pointers which facilitate the execution of selected commands. The shape of some pointers is mostly self-evident, while others, shown below, have the following functions:

↓   The vertical pointer which appears when pointing over a column in a table or worksheet and used to select the column.

→   The horizontal pointer which appears when pointing at a row in a table or worksheet and used to select the row.

◄‖►   The vertical split arrow which appears when pointing over the area separating two columns and used to size a column.

⬍   The horizontal split arrow which appears when pointing over the area separating two rows and used to size a row.

+   The cross which you drag to extend or fill a series.

✐   The draw pointer which appears when you are drawing freehand.

Some Excel operations display a '?' button. Clicking this button changes the mouse pointer from its usual shape to the 'What's this?' shape , as shown here. Pointing with this to an object in the dialogue box or window and left-clicking, gives additional information, as we shall see in the next chapter.

Using the Office Assistant

The Office Assistant is a central source of application information. No matter which Office 2000 application you are using, the Assistant is there to help you.

To find out how it works, start one of the Office applications (we have used Excel), then click the relevant Office Assistant button, shown here, with the left mouse button, type the word *help* in the displayed 'What would you like to do?' box, shown to the left, and left-click the **S**earch button.

A list of help topics is then displayed, as shown to the right. To see more topics, left-click the small triangle at the bottom of the list with the caption 'See more', to display additional topics, as shown below.

To find out how you can use the Office Assistant, click the 'Ways to get assistance while you work' option which causes the display of the screen shown on the next page. From this latter screen you can find out all there is to know about the Office Assistant.

The very same screen can be displayed from all Office applications, with only the title of the window and the 'Finding out what's new in ...' hypertext link, changing to reflect the application in use.

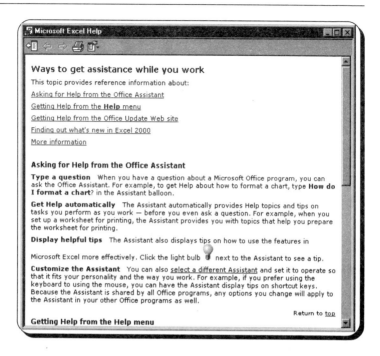

Note the Web browser type buttons at the top of the screen. These allow you to carry out the following functions:

⟨▤	**Show** - click this button to display the help screen tabs which allow you to access Help's Contents, Answer Wizard, and Index.
⇦	**Back** - if more than one help screen has been opened, click this button to go back to the previously opened help screen.
⇨	**Forward** - if you have moved back to a previous help screen, click this button to move forward through opened help screens.
🖨	**Print** - click this button to print the contents of the current help screen.
🖹▾	**Options** - click this button to open up a menu of options which control all of the above facilities plus the ability to select the Internet Options dialogue box.

Customising the Office Assistant

You can customise the Office Assistant to a great degree. Not only can you change the way it responds to your enquiries, but you can also switch it off once you have mastered a particular Office application.

To see the default options settings of the Office Assistant, activate it, left-click on it, and left-click the **Options** button on the displayed box, shown to the right. Doing this, causes the following dialogue box to be displayed on your screen:

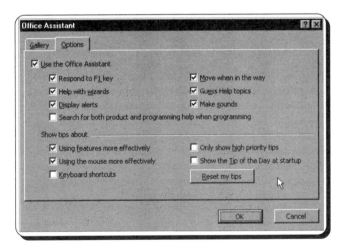

As you can see, it is possible to choose from several options. To change the shape of your Office Assistant (there are eight shapes to choose from - see next page), either left-click the Gallery tab of the above dialogue box, or right-click the Office

Assistant and select the **Choose Assistant** option from the displayed menu, as shown here.

Either action displays the following dialogue box in which you can select your preferred Assistant shape by left-clicking the **Next** button.

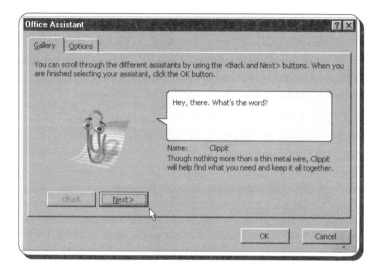

The shapes of the available Assistants are as follows:

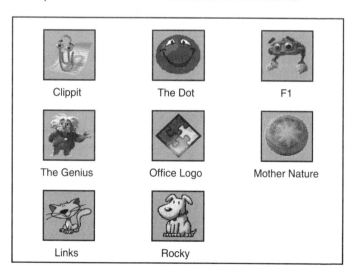

Clippit	The Dot	F1
The Genius	Office Logo	Mother Nature
Links	Rocky	

2

The Excel Environment

Microsoft Excel is a powerful and versatile software package which, over the last few years, has proved its usefulness, not only in the business world, but with scientific and engineering users as well.

The program's power lies in its ability to emulate everything that can be done with a pencil, paper and a calculator. Thus, it is an 'electronic spreadsheet' or simply a 'spreadsheet', a name which is also used to describe it and other similar products. Its power is derived from the power of the computer it is running on, and the flexibility and accuracy with which it can deal with the solution of the various applications it is programmed to manage. These can vary from budgeting and forecasting to the solution of complex scientific and engineering problems.

Starting the Excel Program

Excel is started in Windows either by clicking the **Start** button

then selecting **Programs** and clicking on the 'Microsoft Excel' icon on the cascade menu, clicking the Excel icon on the Office Shortcut Bar, or the 'Open Office Document' icon on the Office Shortcut Bar, or by double-clicking on an Excel workbook file. In the latter case the workbook will be loaded into Excel at the same time.

Whether you have used a previous version of Excel or not, the first time you use the program, it might be a good idea to activate **The Office Assistant** and type *what's new* in the text box, then click **Search**.

This displays the following Help screen. Start by looking at the 'Key information for upgraders and new users' option, from which you can find out differences between this version of Excel and previous versions of the program. Then, look at the 'What's new in Microsoft Excel 2000' option.

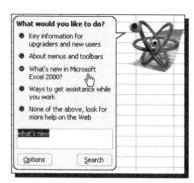

We suggest you spend a little time here browsing through the various help screens. Below, we show the help topics available under 'What's new in Microsoft Excel 2000' so that you can see the wealth of information contained in them.

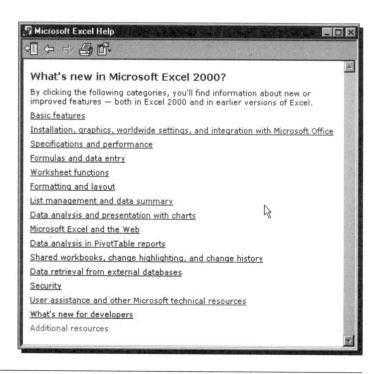

What's new in Microsoft Excel 2000?

By clicking the following categories, you'll find information about new or improved features — both in Excel 2000 and in earlier versions of Excel.

Basic features

Installation, graphics, worldwide settings, and integration with Microsoft Office

Specifications and performance

Formulas and data entry

Worksheet functions

Formatting and layout

List management and data summary

Data analysis and presentation with charts

Microsoft Excel and the Web

Data analysis in PivotTable reports

Shared workbooks, change highlighting, and change history

Data retrieval from external databases

Security

User assistance and other Microsoft technical resources

What's new for developers

Additional resources

The Excel Screen

When Excel is loaded, a 'blank' spreadsheet screen displays with a similar Title bar, Menu bar, Toolbar and Formatting bar to those of Word. Obviously there are some differences, but that is to be expected as the two programs serve different purposes.

The opening screen of Excel is shown below. It is perhaps worth looking at the various parts that make up this screen, or window. Excel follows the usual Microsoft Windows conventions which hopefully you should be familiar with by now.

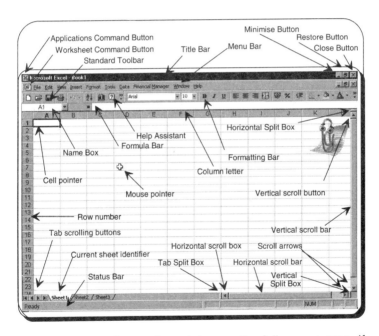

The window as shown above takes up the full screen area. If you click on the application restore button, the top one of the two restore buttons at the top right of the screen, you can make Excel show in a smaller window. This can be useful when you are running several applications at the same time and you want to transfer between them with the mouse.

Note that in this case, the Excel window displays an empty document with the title 'Book1', and has a solid 'Title bar', indicating that it is the active application window. Although multiple windows can be displayed simultaneously, you can only enter data into the active window (which will always be displayed on top). Title bars of non-active windows appear a lighter shade than that of the active one.

The Excel screen is divided into several areas which have identical functions to other Microsoft Office applications. Below, we describe first the areas that are common to other Office programs, and then those that are exclusive to Excel.

Area	*Function*
Command buttons	Clicking on the command button, (upper-left corner of the Excel window), displays a pull-down menu which can be used to control the program window. You can restore, move, size, minimise, maximise, and close the window.
Title Bar	The bar at the top of a window which displays the application name and the name of the current document.
Minimise Button	When clicked on, it minimises a document, or the application to an icon on the Windows Taskbar.
Restore Button	When clicked on, it restores the active window to the position and size that was occupied before it was maximised. The restore button is then replaced by a Maximise button, shown here, which is used to maximise the window.

Close button	The extreme top right button that you click to close a window.
Menu Bar	The bar below the Title bar which allows you to choose from several menu options. Clicking on a menu item displays the pull-down menu associated with that item.
Standard Toolbar	The bar below the Menu bar which contains buttons that give you mouse click access to the functions most often used in the program. These are grouped according to function.
Formatting Bar	The buttons on the Formatting Bar which allow you to change the attributes of a font, such as italic and bold, and also to format text and numbers in various ways. The Formatting Bar contains two boxes; a font box and a size box which show the font and size of characters currently being used. These boxes give access to other installed fonts and character sizes.
Split Boxes	Excel has two split boxes, the horizontal and vertical split boxes. The first is located at the extreme right of the screen above the 'top vertical scroll arrow' button. The second is located at the extreme bottom-right corner of the screen, to the left of the 'right horizontal scroll arrow' button. Dragging these buttons allows you to split the screen either horizontally or vertically.

Scroll Bars	The vertical and horizontal areas on the screen that contain scroll boxes. Clicking on these bars allows you to see parts of a document which are not visible on the screen.
Scroll Arrows	The arrowheads at each end of each scroll bar at which you can click to scroll the screen up and down one line, or left and right 10% of the screen, at a time.
Status Bar	The bottom line of the document window that displays status information.
Name box	Identifies the selected cell (by name or by cell co-ordinates), chart item, or drawing object.
Formula Bar	Can display a number, a label, or the formula behind a result.
Cell pointer	Marks the current cell.
Column letter	The letter that identifies a column.
Row number	The number that identifies a row.
Tab scrolling	Clicking on these buttons, scrolls sheet tabs right or left, when there are more tabs than can be displayed at once.
Current sheet	Shows the current sheet amongst a number of sheets in a file. These are named Sheet1, Sheet2, and so on, by default, but can be changed to, say, North, and South. Clicking on a sheet tab, moves you to that sheet.
Tab split box	The split box which you drag left to see more of the scroll bar, or right to see more tabs.

The Standard Toolbar

This is located below the Menu bar at the top of the Excel screen and contains command buttons. If either the Standard

toolbar or the Formatting bar are not displayed on your screen, use the **View, Toolbars** command to open up a menu of options, as shown to the left. You can toggle these on and off by clicking on their names.

To action a command, left-click its button with the mouse. Not only can you control what buttons show on the various toolbars, but as you work with Excel the buttons you use most often are displayed on them automatically. When you first start Excel, the following command buttons are displayed on the Standard toolbar:

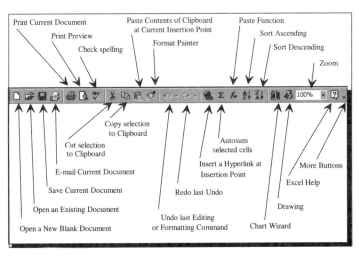

Using these Standard Toolbar buttons will be discussed in detail, with worked examples, in this and following chapters.

The Formatting Bar

This is located below the Standard Toolbar, and is divided into sections that contain command buttons, as shown below.

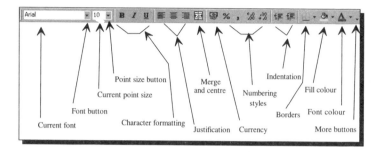

The Current font box shows the current typeface. Clicking on the down-arrow button to the right of it allows you to change the typeface of any selected text. The Current point size box shows the size of selected characters which can be changed by clicking on the down-arrow button next to it and selecting another size from the displayed list.

Next, are three character formatting buttons which allow you to enhance selected text by emboldening, italicising, or underlining it. The next three buttons allow you to change the justification of characters in selected cells, and the next button allows you to merge selected cells and have their contents centred. The next seven buttons help you set the different types of Numbering and Indentation options. The last three buttons allow you to add Borders to selected cells or objects, fill them with colour, or change the font colour of selected characters.

Clicking on the More Buttons arrow, opens up the **Add or Remove Buttons** option which when activated displays all the available buttons for that toolbar. The ones displayed on the toolbar are shown ticked, but there are additional ones not displayed on the tollbar, as shown to the right.

The Menu Bar Options

Each menu bar option has associated with it a pull-down sub-menu. To activate the menu, either press the <Alt> key, which causes the first option of the menu (in this case the **File** menu option) to be selected, then use the right and left arrow keys to highlight any of the options in the menu, or use the mouse to point to an option. Pressing either the <Enter> key, or the left mouse button, reveals the pull-down sub-menu of the highlighted menu option. The sub-menu of the **File** option is shown below.

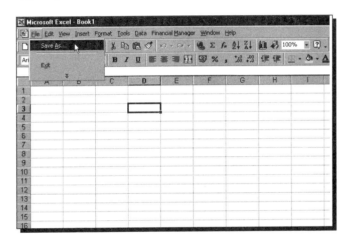

Note that in this version of Excel, the drop-down sub-menu displays only the most important options, but you have the option to view the full sub-menu by highlighting the double arrow-heads at the bottom of it, by either pointing to that part of the sub-menu with the mouse or using the down-arrow cursor key to move the highlighted bar down.

The full sub-menu of the **File** menu option is displayed on the next page. However, the order of the sub-menu options in both the short and the full version of the sub-menu could differ from ours. This is because Excel, and the other Office 2000 applications, now learn from your actions and automatically promote the items you choose from menu extensions on to the shortened version of the sub-menu.

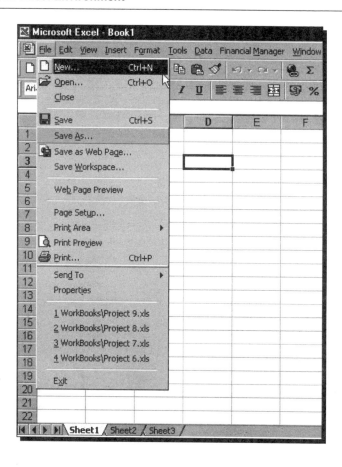

Menu options can also be activated directly by pressing the <Alt> key followed by the underlined letter of the required option. Thus, pressing <Alt+F>, causes the pull-down **File** sub-menu to be displayed. You can use the up and down arrow keys to move the highlighted bar up and down a sub-menu, or the right and left arrow keys to move along the options in the menu bar. Pressing the <Enter> key selects the highlighted option or executes the highlighted command. Pressing the <Esc> key once, closes the pull-down sub-menu, while pressing the <Esc> key for a second time, closes the menu system.

Some of the sub-menu options can be accessed with 'quick key' combinations from the keyboard. Such combinations are shown on the drop-down menus, for example, <Ctrl+S> is the quick key for the **Save** option in the **File** sub-menu. If a sub-menu option is not available, at any time, it will display in a grey colour. Some menu options only appear in Excel when that tool is being used, but the ones described below remain constant.

The following is a brief description of the standard menu options. For a more detailed description of each sub-menu item, use the on-line **Help** system.

File   Produces a pull-down menu of mainly file related tasks, such as creating a **New** Workbook, the ability to **Open**, or **Close** files, and **Save** files with the same name, or **Save As** a different name, or even **Save as Web Page**. You can use **Page Setup** to set the margins and the size of your printed page, **Set/Clear Print Area**, **Print Preview** a document on screen before committing it to paper, **Print** a document and select your current printer. You can also direct documents to other users who share resources with you, using the **Send To** option, view a specific file's **Properties**, and **Exit** the program. Above this last option, Excel also displays the last four documents you used so that you can open them easily.

Edit   Produces a pull-down menu which allows you to **Undo** changes made, **Cut**, **Copy** and **Paste** cell entries, graphics, as **Links** or **Hyperlinks**, **Fill** cells in specific directions, **Clear** entries and formats, **Delete** cell contents, rows or columns, **Delete, Move or Copy Sheets**, **Find** specific text or formulae in a worksheet, **Find and Replace** text or values, jump to any location in a worksheet, view and update **Links**, or open a selected **Object**.

V̲iew   Produces a pull-down menu which contains
                        screen display options which allow you to
                        change the editing view to **Normal**, or **Page
                        Break Preview**. You can further control
                        whether to display the **Toolbars**, **Formula
                        Bar**, or **Status Bar**, show a list of
                        Headers/Footers, open windows for
                        viewing **Comments**, display a **Full Screen**,
                        and determine the scale of the editing view
                        by using the **Zoom** option.

I̲nsert   Produces a pull-down menu which allows
                        you to insert **Cells, Rows, Columns,
                        Worksheet, Chart,** and **Page Break**. You
                        can also insert a **Function**, a range **Name**,
                        a **Comment**, a **Picture**, or an **Object** into
                        the active worksheet, or insert **Hyperlinks** to
                        other documents.

Fo̲rmat   Produces a pull-down menu which allows
                        you to alter the appearance of entries in
                        selected **Cells**, a **Row**, a **Column**, or an
                        active **Sheet**. You can further select options
                        to **AutoFormat** a worksheet, and select or
                        modify a **Style**.

T̲ools   Produces a pull-down menu that gives
                        access to the **Spelling** checker, and add or
                        delete **AutoCorrect** entries. You can also
                        give permission to **Share a Workbook,
                        Track Changes** made to it, and **Protect**
                        specified worksheets or workbooks, and
                        activate **Online Collaboration**. Further, you
                        can use **Goal Seek** to fine-tune a formula to
                        give you the required result, examine
                        different what-if **Scenarios**, or use the
                        Auditing option to analyse the way your
                        worksheet is structured. Finally, you can run,
                        create, delete or edit a **Macro** (a set of
                        instructions), **Customize** Excel to your
                        requirements and change various Excel
                        Options.

<u>D</u>ata	You can **Sort** selected data in ascending or descending order, use the **Filter** option to hide data, or copy data to another location on a worksheet, if they do not meet the specified criteria. You can also use a **Form** to enter or edit data, create **Subtotals**, or use the **Data Validation** option to apply restrictions on data entry to selected cells. Further, you can use the **Table** option to calculate and display the results of substituting different values for one or more variables in a formula, or you can select a section of text and use the **Convert Text to Table** option to have it incorporated within a worksheet. Finally, you can specify the range of data to **Consolidate** with other source areas, use the **Pivot Table and Pivot Chart Report** wizard to create an interactive table or chart that summarises your data, or **Get External Data** by running a query.
F. <u>M</u>anager	The Small business Financial Manager lets you make informed business decisions using several reporting and analysis tools built on top of Microsoft Excel.
<u>W</u>indow	Allows you to open a **New Window**, and control the display of existing open windows on the screen. You can also **Hide** or **Split** worksheets, or **Freeze Panes**.
<u>H</u>elp	Allows you to access the **Microsoft Excel Help**, **Hide the Office Assistant**, the **What's This** facility, or the **Office on the Web** option (if you are connected to the Internet). You can also get help if you are a **Lotus 1-2-3** user, **Detect and Repair** errors in Excel, or use the **About Microsoft Excel** option to find out information about your system, or get information on Technical Support.

Shortcut Menus

As with the three previous versions of Excel you can use context-sensitive shortcut menus. If you click the right mouse button on any screen, or document, a shortcut menu is displayed with the most frequently used commands relating to the type of work you were doing at the time.

The composite screen dump below shows in turn the shortcut menus that open when a cell is selected, or either of the Toolbars is selected.

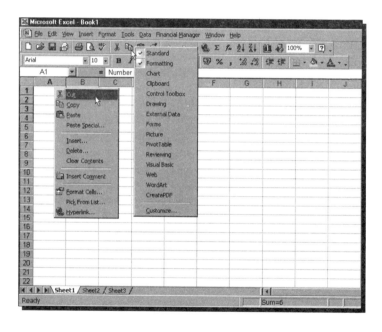

So, whatever you are doing in Excel, you have rapid access to a menu of relevant functions by right-clicking your mouse. Left-clicking the mouse at a menu selection will choose that function, while right-clicking on an area outside the shortcut menu (or pressing the <Esc> key), closes down the shortcut menu.

Dialogue Boxes

Three periods after a sub-menu option or command, means that a dialogue box will open when the option or command is selected. A dialogue box is used for the insertion of additional information, such as the name of a file or path.

To see a dialogue box, press <Alt+F>, and select the **Open** option. The 'Open' dialogue box is displayed, as shown below.

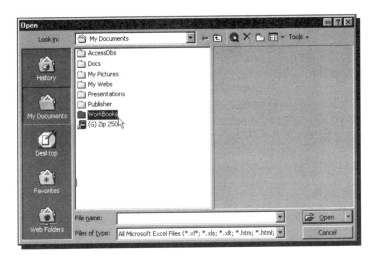

When a dialogue box opens, the easiest way to move around it is by clicking with the mouse, otherwise the <Tab> key can be used to move the cursor from one column in the box to another (<Shift+Tab> moves the cursor backwards). Alternatively you can move directly to a desired field by holding the <Alt> key down and pressing the underlined letter in the field name.

Within a column of options you must use the arrow keys to move from one to another. Having selected an option or typed in information, you must press a command button such as the **Open** or **Cancel** button, or choose from additional options.

To select the **Open** button with the mouse, simply point and click, while with the keyboard you must first press the <Tab> key until the dotted rectangle, or focus, moves to the required button, and then press the <Enter> key. Pressing <Enter> at any time while a dialogue box is open, will cause the marked items to be selected and the box to be closed.

Some dialogue boxes contain List boxes which show a column of available choices, similar to the one at the top of the previous screen dump which appears by pressing the down-arrow button, as shown below.

If there are more choices than can be seen in the area provided, use the scroll bars to reveal them. To select a single item from a List box, either double-click the item, or use the arrow keys to highlight the item and press <Enter>.

Some dialogue boxes contain Option buttons with a list of mutually exclusive items. The default choice is marked with a black dot against its name, while unavailable options are dimmed. Other dialogue boxes contain Check boxes which offer a list of options you can switch on or off. Selected options show a tick in the box against the option name, while incompatible options appear greyed out. If you want to see an example of these types of dialogue boxes, use the **Window, Arrange** command to open the Arrange Windows dialogue box.

To cancel a dialogue box, either click the **Cancel** button, or press the <Esc> key. Pressing the <Esc> key in succession, closes one dialogue box at a time, and eventually aborts the menu option.

Using the Help Menu

Another way of getting help in
Excel (apart from using the Office
Assistant), is to use the **F1**
function key to get directly to the
Context and Index help screens.
To do so, however, you will first
have to switch off the Office
Assistant by right-clicking it and
selecting **Options** from the

drop-down menu. This opens the following dialogue box, in
which you must clear the box against **Use the Office
Assistant**, as shown below.

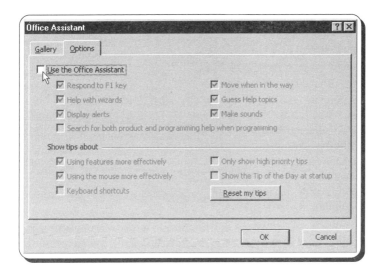

Next time you press the **F1** function key, the Office Help
screen appears as shown on the next page. You can either
view information on the screen or print it on paper.
Left-clicking the Index tab, displays a dialogue box with three
areas for typing, selecting and displaying information, as
shown.

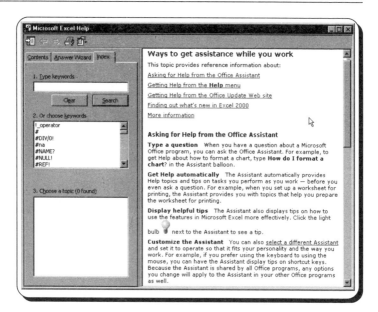

Typing, for example, the words **find fast** in the first 'Type keywords' box, causes a list of related topics to appear automatically in the second 'Or choose key words' box. Selecting one or more matching words from the displayed list narrows down the selection of topics appearing in the third 'Choose a topic' box. Finally, selecting a topic from the third display box by left-clicking it, displays information on your selection.

If the keyword you want to choose is not visible within the display area of the second box, use the scroll bar to get to it.

As an exercise, click the Answer Wizard tab of the Help dialogue box and type the words 'backward compatibility' in the 'What would you like to do' box and click the **Search** button. Highlighting the fourth topic of the list in the second text box, 'About using Microsoft Excel 2000 files with earlier versions of Excel', displays information on the topic in the right-hand pane, as shown on the next page. As each topic in this list is selected, information about it is automatically displayed.

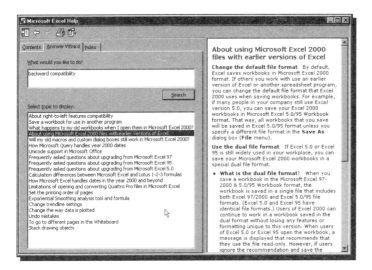

The displayed information in the right-hand pane of the above Excel Help screen will tell you all you need to know regarding file formats. Similar searches carried out from other Office 2000 applications will reveal what you should do if you require backward compatibility.

It is worth while exploring the different ways in which you  can get help with or without the Office Assistant. For example, another way of getting context sensitive help is to select the '**What's This?**' option from the extended **Help** sub-menu, then move the modified mouse pointer to an area of the document, or onto a particular Toolbar button, or menu item, and press the left mouse button.

Finally, click the Contents tab of the Help screen to open up an impressive list of topics relating to the Excel 2000 program. Left-clicking a selected book, displays the topics and other books it might contain. As each topic is selected, information about that topic appears on the adjacent screen, as shown overleaf.

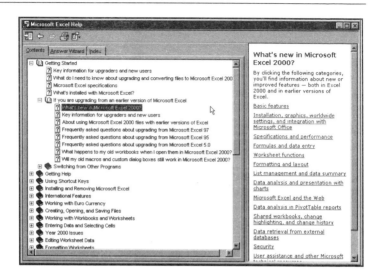

Note the small '+' signs to the left of each book. Left-clicking this sign, opens up the relevant book, indicated by a '-' sign. Do spend some time here to learn, particularly what is new in Excel. Other topics can always be explored later.

3

The Excel Spreadsheet

When you first enter Excel, the program sets up a series of huge electronic pages, or worksheets, in your computer's memory, many times larger than the small part shown on the screen. Individual cells are identified by column and row location (in that order), with present size extending to 256 columns and 65,536 rows. The columns are labelled from A to Z, followed by AA to AZ, BA to BZ, and so on, to IV, while the rows are numbered from 1 to 65,536.

A worksheet can be thought of as a two-dimensional table made up of rows and columns. The point where a row and column intersect is called a cell, while the reference points of a cell are known as the cell address. The active cell (A1 when you first enter the program) is boxed.

Workbook Navigation

Navigation around the worksheet is achieved by using one of the following keys or key combinations:

- Pressing one of the four arrow keys ($\rightarrow\downarrow\leftarrow\uparrow$) moves the active cell one position right, down, left or up, respectively.

- Pressing the <PgDn> or <PgUp> keys moves the active cell down or up one visible page.

- Pressing the <Ctrl+$\rightarrow$> or <Ctrl+$\downarrow$> key combinations moves the active cell to the extreme right of the worksheet (column IV) or extreme bottom of the worksheet (row 65,536).

- Pressing the <Home> key, moves the active cell to the beginning of a row.

- Pressing the <Ctrl+Home> key combination moves the active cell to the home position, A1.

- Pressing the <Ctrl+End> key combination moves the active cell to the lower right corner of the worksheet's currently used area.

- Pressing the **F5** function key will display the Go To dialogue box shown below.

In the **Go to** box a list of named ranges in the active worksheet (to be discussed shortly) is displayed, or one of the last four references from which you chose the **Go To** command.

In the **Reference** box you type the cell reference or a named range you want to move to.

To move the active cell with a mouse, do the following:

- Point to the cell you want to move to and click the left mouse button. If the cell is not visible, move the window by clicking on the scroll bar arrowhead that points in the direction you want to move,

- To move a page at a time, click in the scroll bar itself.

- For larger moves, drag the box in the scroll bar, but the distances moved will depend on the size of the worksheet.

When you have finished navigating around the worksheet, press the <Ctrl+Home> key combination which will move the active cell to the A1 position (provided you have not fixed titles in any rows or columns or have no hidden rows or columns - more about these later).

Note that the area within which you can move the active cell is referred to as the working area of the worksheet, while the letters and numbers in the border at the top and left of the working area give the 'co-ordinates' of the cells.

The location of the active cell is constantly monitored by the 'selection indicator' which is to be found on the extreme left below the lower Toolbar of the application window. As the active cell is moved, this indicator displays its address, as shown below.

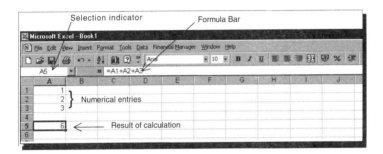

The contents of a cell are displayed above the column letters within what is known as the 'Formula Bar'. If you type text in the active cell, what you type appears in both the Formula Bar and the cell itself.

Typing a formula which is preceded by the equals sign (=) to, say, add the contents of three cells, causes the actual formula to appear in the Formula Bar, while the result of the actual calculation appears in the active cell when the <Enter> key is pressed.

Moving Between Sheets

You can scroll between sheets by clicking one of the arrows situated to the left of Sheet1, as shown on the next page. We have labelled these as 'Tab scrolling buttons'. The inner arrows scroll sheets one at a time in the direction of the arrow, while the outer arrows scroll to the end, or beginning, of the group of available sheets. A sheet is then made current by clicking its tab.

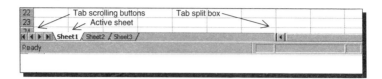

With the keyboard, you can scroll one sheet at a time, and make it active at the same time, by using the <Ctrl+PgDn> key combination. Using <Ctrl+PgUp> scrolls in the reverse direction.

To display more sheet tabs at a time, drag the split box to the right. The reverse action displays less sheet tabs. To rename sheets, double-click at their tab, then type a new name to replace the highlighted name of the particular sheet tab.

To insert a sheet in front of a certain sheet, make that sheet current, then use the **Insert, Worksheet** command sequence. To delete a sheet, make it current and use the **Edit, Delete Sheet** command sequence.

Rearranging Sheet Order

If you need to rearrange the order in which sheets are being held in a workbook, you can do so by dragging a particular sheet's tab to its new position, as shown below.

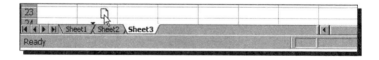

While you are dragging the tab of the sheet you want to move, the mouse pointer changes to an arrow pointing to a sheet. The small solid arrowhead to the left of the mouse pointer indicates the place where the sheet you are moving will be placed, when you release the mouse button.

Grouping Worksheets

You can select several sheets to group them together so that data entry, editing, or formatting can be made easier and more consistent.

To select adjacent sheets, click the first sheet tab, hold down the <Shift> key and then click the last sheet tab in the group. To select non-adjacent sheets, click the first sheet tab, hold down the <Ctrl> key and then click the other sheet tabs you want to group together.

Selecting sheets in the above manner, causes the word '[Group]' to appear in the Title bar of the active window, and the tabs of the selected sheets to be shown in white. To cancel the selection, click at the tab of any sheet which is not part of the selected group.

Selecting a Range of Cells

To select a range of cells, say, A3:C3, point to cell A3, then

- press the left mouse button, and while holding it pressed, drag the mouse to the right.

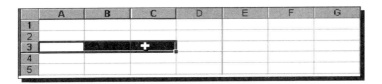

To select a range from the keyboard, first make active the first cell in the range, then

- hold down the <Shift> key and use the right arrow key (→) to highlight the required range.

To select a 3D range, across several sheets, select the range in the first sheet, then

- release the mouse button, hold down the <Shift> key, and click the Tab of the last sheet in the range.

Viewing Multiple Workbook Sheets

To see more clearly what you are doing when working with multiple workbook sheets, type the text '1st' in location A1 of Sheet1, the text '2nd' in Sheet2, and so on (to add extra sheets in a workbook, use the **Insert, Worksheet** command). Then use the **Window, New Window** command to add three extra windows to your worksheet. Next, use the **Window, Arrange, Tiled** command to display the four sheets as shown below. What we have done below is to make active Sheet1 in Book1:1, Sheet2 in Book1:2, and so on, to demonstrate that each window contains all four sheets.

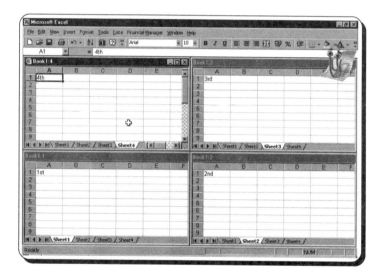

To move from one window to another, simply point with the mouse to the cell of the window you want to go to and click the left mouse button. To display a different sheet in each window, go to a window and click the sheet's tab.

To return to single-window view mode from a tiled or cascade mode, click the maximise button of the active window.

Entering Information

We will now investigate how information can be entered into a worksheet. But first, make sure you are in Sheet1, then return to the Home (A1) position, by pressing the <Ctrl+Home> key combination, then type the words:

```
Project Analysis
```

As you type, the characters appear in both the 'Formula Bar' and the active cell. If you make a mistake, press the <BkSp> key to erase the previous letter or the <Esc> key to start again. When you have finished, press <Enter>.

Note that what you have just typed in has been entered in cell A1, even though the whole of the word ANALYSIS appears to be in cell B1. If you use the right arrow key to move the active cell to B1 you will see that the cell is indeed empty.

Typing any letter at the beginning of an entry into a cell results in a 'text' entry being formed automatically, otherwise known as a 'label'. If the length of the text is longer than the width of a cell, it will continue into the next cell to the right of the current active cell, provided that cell is empty, otherwise the displayed information will be truncated.

To edit information already in a cell, either

* double-click the cell in question, or

* make that cell the active cell and press the **F2** function key.

The cursor keys, the <Home> and <End> keys, as well as the <Ins> and <Del> keys can then be used to move the cursor and/or edit information as required.

You can also 'undo' the last 16 actions carried out since the program was last in the **Ready** mode, by either using the **Edit, Undo Entry** command (<Ctrl+Z>), or clicking the Undo button.

Next, move the active cell to B3 and type

```
Jan
```

Pressing the right arrow key (→) will automatically enter the typed information into the cell and also move the active cell one cell to the right, in this case to C3. Now type

```
Feb
```

and press <Enter>.

The looks of a worksheet can be enhanced somewhat by using different types of borders around specific cells. To do this, first select the range of cells, then click at the down arrow of the Borders icon on the Formatting Toolbar, shown here, which displays twelve different types of borders, as shown below.

In our example, we have selected the cell range A3:C3, then we chose the 8th border from the display table.

Next, move to cell A4 and type the label Income, then enter the numbers 14000 and 15000 in cells B4 and C4, respectively, as shown below, but note that by default the labels 'Jan' and 'Feb' are left justified, while the numbers are right justified.

	A	B	C	D	E	F	G	H
1	PROJECT ANALYSIS							
2								
3		Jan	Feb					
4	Income	14000	15000					
5								

Changing Text Alignment and Fonts

One way of improving the looks of this worksheet is to also right justify the text 'Jan' and 'Feb' within their respective cells. To do this, move the active cell to B3 and select the range B3 to C3 by dragging the mouse, then either click the 'Align Right' icon, shown here, or choose the **Format**, **Cells** command, then select the **Alignment** tab from the displayed Format Cells dialogue box, shown below, click the down-arrow against the **Horizontal** text box, highlight **Right** from the drop-down menu options, and press **OK**.

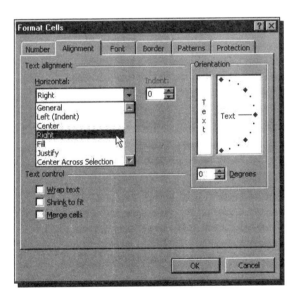

No matter which method you choose, the text should now appear right justified within their cells. However, although the latter method is lengthier, it nevertheless provides you with greater flexibility in displaying text, both in terms of position and orientation.

We could further improve the looks of our worksheet by choosing a different font for the heading 'Project Analysis'. To achieve this, select cell A1, then click on the down arrow against the Font Size button on the Formatting Bar, to reveal the band of available point sizes for the selected font. From this band, choose 14, then click in succession the 'Bold' and 'Italic' icons.

Finally, since the numbers in cells B4 to C4 represent money, it would be better if these were prefixed with the £ sign. To do this, select the cell range B4:C4, then either click the 'Currency' button on the Formatting Bar, shown here, or choose the **Format, Style** command and select **Currency** from the list under **Style name** in the displayed Style dialogue box.

The numbers within the chosen range will now be displayed in currency form, and the width of the cells will automatically adjust to accommodate them, if they are too long which is the case in our example.

To see the actual new width of, say column C, place the mouse pointer, as shown, to the right of the column letter on the dividing line. When the mouse pointer changes to the

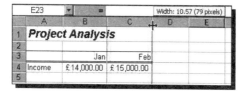

shape shown here, press the left mouse button. The current width will then display within a pop-up text box as 79 pixels, increased from the default column width of 64 pixels.

This new width accommodates our numbers exactly, but we might like to increase it to, say, 82 pixels so that it looks better. To do this, place the mouse pointer in between the column letters, and drag the pointer to the right, until the width of the column displays as 82 pixels, which also happens to be 11 characters wide.

Saving a Workbook

Now, let us assume that we would like to stop at this point, but would also like to save the work entered so far before leaving the program. First, return to the Home position by pressing <Ctrl+Home>. This is good practice because the position of the cell pointer at the time of saving the file is preserved. For example, had you placed the cell pointer well beyond the data entry area of your worksheet at the time of saving, when you later opened this worksheet you might be confused to see empty cells surrounding the cell pointer - you might think that you have opened an empty worksheet.

Next, choose the **File, Save** command to reveal the Save As dialogue box. You could select to save your work in the default **My Documents** folder, or create a suitably named folder using the Create New Folder button on the Save As dialogue box, shown below.

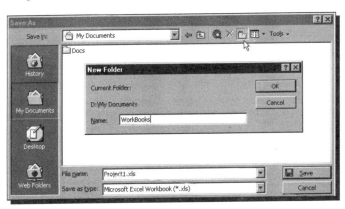

We used this facility to create a folder called **WorkBooks** within the **My Documents** folder.

To save our work currently in memory, we selected the **WorkBooks** folder in the **Save in** field of the Save As dialogue box, then moved the cursor into the **File name** box, and typed **Project 1**. We suggest you do the same.

The file will be saved in the default file type *Microsoft Excel Workbook*, as displayed in the **Save as type** box. Excel adds the file extension **.xls** automatically and uses it to identify it.

By clicking the **Save as type** button at the bottom of the Save As dialogue box, you can save your work in a variety of other formats, including Web Page (HTML), Template, and earlier versions of Excel.

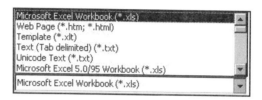

If you want to create backup files or provide password protection to your file, click the down-arrow against the **Tools** button at the top of the Save As dialogue box, and select **General Options** from the displayed drop down menu. This opens the Save Options dialogue box, shown in the middle of the composite screen dump below. Fill in this dialogue box appropriately and press the **OK** button.

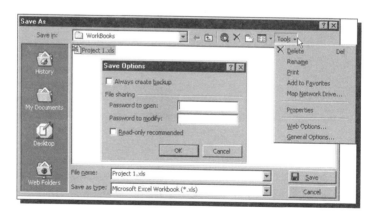

Finally, pressing the **Save** button causes your work to be saved under the chosen filename.

Opening a Workbook

 An already saved workbook, or file, can be opened by either clicking at the 'Open' icon, shown here, or selecting the **File, Open** command which displays the Open dialogue box. Excel asks for a filename to open, with the default *Microsoft Excel Files* being displayed in the **Files of type** box, as shown below. If the file was saved, select it by clicking its name in the list box, then click the **Open** button.

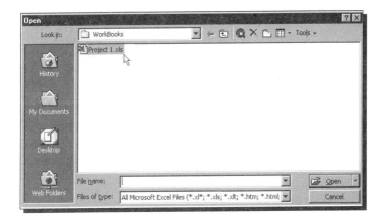

If you haven't saved it, don't worry as you could just as easily start afresh.

If you want to change the logged drive, click the down-arrow against the **Look in** box, of the Open dialogue box, and select the appropriate drive from the drop-down list, as shown here for our computer. In your case, this list will most certainly be different.

Exiting Excel

To exit Excel, close any displayed dialogue boxes by clicking the **Cancel** button, and make sure that the word **Ready** is displayed on the status bar (press the <Esc> key until it does), and either

- choose the **File, Exit** command,
- use the <Alt+F4> key combination, or
- click the **Close** button.

No matter which command you choose, if you have changed any opened worksheet, Excel will warn you and will ask for confirmation before exiting the program, as follows.

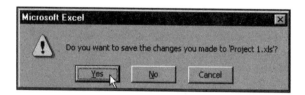

If you do not want to save the changes, then press the **No** button, otherwise press **Yes**.

4

Filling in a Worksheet

We will use, as an example of how a worksheet can be built up, the few entries on 'Project Analysis' from the previous chapter. If you have saved **Project 1**, then either click the Open button, or use the **File, Open** command, then highlight its filename in the Open dialogue box, and click the **OK** button. If you haven't saved it, don't worry as you could just as easily start afresh.

Next, either double-click on the contents of a cell to edit existing entries, or simply retype the contents of cells, so that your worksheet looks as near as possible to the one below. For formatting details, see below and the next page.

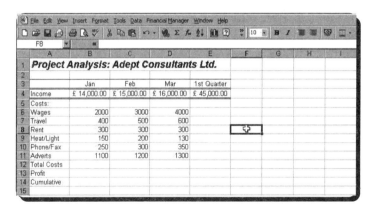

 The lines, like the double line stretching from A3 to E3 were entered by first selecting the cell range A3:E3, then clicking the down-arrow of the 'Borders' icon on the Formatting Bar, and selecting the appropriate border from the 12 displayed options.

Formatting Entries

The information in cell A1 (Project Analysis: Adept Consultants Ltd.) was entered left justified and formatted by clicking on the 'Font Size' button on the Formatting Bar, and

  selecting 14 point font size from the band of available font sizes, then clicking in succession the 'Bold' and 'Italic' icons, shown to the left.

The text in the cell block B3:E3 was formatted by first

 selecting the range and then clicking the 'Centre' alignment icon on the Formatting Bar, so the text within the range was displayed centre justified.

The numbers within the cell block B4:E4 were formatted by first selecting the range, then clicking the 'Currency' icon on

the Formatting Bar, shown here, so the numbers appeared with two digits after the decimal point and prefixed with the £ sign.

All the text appearing in column A (apart from that in cell A1) was just typed in (left justified), as shown in the screen dump on the previous page. The width of all the columns A to E was adjusted to 11 characters; a quick way of doing this is to select one row of these columns, then use the **Format, Column, Width** command, and type 11 in the displayed box.

Filling a Range by Example

To fill a range by example, select the first cell of a range,

 point at the bottom right corner of the cell and when the mouse pointer changes to a small cross, drag the mouse in the required direction to fill the range.

In the above case, we started with a cell containing the abbreviation 'Jan'. The next cell to the right will automatically fill with the text 'Feb' (Excel anticipates that you want to fill cells by example with the abbreviations for months, and does it for you). Not only that, but it also copies the format of the selected range forward.

Entering Text, Numbers and Formulae

Excel allows you to format both text (labels) and numbers in any way you choose. For example, you can have numbers centre justified in their cells. When text, a number, a formula, or an Excel function is entered into a cell, or reference is made to the contents of a cell by the cell address, then the content of the status bar changes from **Ready** to **Enter**. This status can be changed back to **Ready** by either completing an entry and pressing <Enter> or one of the arrow keys, or by pressing <Esc>.

We can find the 1st quarter total income from consultancy, by activating cell E4, typing

=b4+c4+d4

and pressing <Enter>. The total first quarter income is added, using the above formula, and the result is placed in cell E4.

Now complete the insertion into the spreadsheet of the various amounts under 'costs' and then choose the **File, Save As** command to save the resultant worksheet under the filename **Project 2**, before going on any further. Remember that saving your work on disc often enough is a good thing to get used to, as even the shortest power cut can cause the loss of hours of hard work!

Using Functions

In our example, writing a formula that adds the contents of three columns is not too difficult or lengthy a task. But imagine having to add 20 columns! For this reason Excel has an inbuilt summation function which can be used to add any number of columns (or rows).

To illustrate how this and other functions can be used, activate cell E4 and first press <Del> to clear the cell of its formula, then click the Paste Function button, shown here, on the Standard Toolbar. If the function you require appears on the displayed dialogue box under **Function name**, choose it, otherwise select the appropriate class from the list under **Function category**.

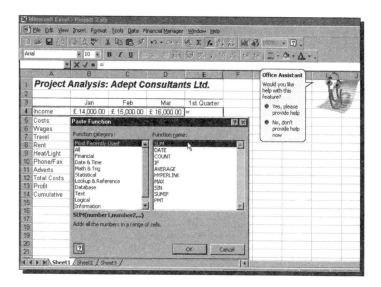

Choosing the **SUM** function, inserts the entry SUM(B4:D4) in the Edit line, as shown below. Clicking the **OK** button, causes this function to be pasted into cell E4, adding all the numbers in the range.

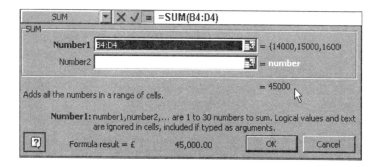

Using the AutoSum Icon

With addition, there is a better and quicker way of letting Excel work out the desired result. To illustrate this, select the cell range B6:E12, which contains the 'Costs' we would like to add up. To add these in both the horizontal and vertical direction, we include in the selected range an empty column to the right of the numbers and an empty row below the numbers, as shown below.

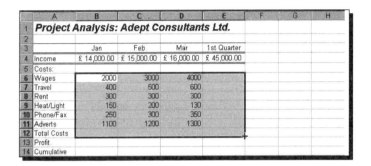

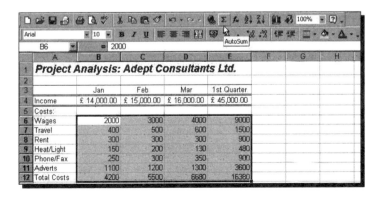

Pressing the 'AutoSum' icon, shown here, inserts the result of the summations in the empty column and row, as shown below. The selected range remains selected so that any other formatting can be applied by simply pressing the appropriate icon button.

Now complete the insertion of formulae in the rest of the worksheet, noting that 'Profit', in B13, is the difference between 'Income' and 'Total Cost', calculated by the formula **=b4-b12**. To complete the entry, this formula should be copied using the 'fill by example' method into the three cells to its right.

The 'Cumulative' entry in cell B14 should be a simple reference to cell B13, that is **+b13**, while in cell C14 it should be **=b14+b13**. Similarly, the latter formula is copied into cell D14 using the 'fill by example' method.

Next, format the entire range B6:E12 by selecting the range and clicking the 'Currency' button.

If you make any mistakes and copy formats or information into cells you did not mean to, use the **Edit, Undo** command, or click the Undo button which allows you to selectively undo what you were just doing. To blank the contents within a range of cells, first select the range, then press the <Del> key.

The worksheet, up to this point, should look as follows:

	A	B	C	D	E	F	G	H
1	**Project Analysis: Adept Consultants Ltd.**							
2								
3		Jan	Feb	Mar	1st Quarter			
4	Income	£ 14,000.00	£ 15,000.00	£ 16,000.00	£ 45,000.00			
5	Costs:							
6	Wages	£ 2,000.00	£ 3,000.00	£ 4,000.00	£ 9,000.00			
7	Travel	£ 400.00	£ 500.00	£ 600.00	£ 1,500.00			
8	Rent	£ 300.00	£ 300.00	£ 300.00	£ 900.00		⇩	
9	Heat/Light	£ 150.00	£ 200.00	£ 130.00	£ 480.00			
10	Phone/Fax	£ 250.00	£ 300.00	£ 350.00	£ 900.00			
11	Adverts	£ 1,100.00	£ 1,200.00	£ 1,300.00	£ 3,600.00			
12	Total Costs	£ 4,200.00	£ 5,500.00	£ 6,680.00	£ 16,380.00			
13	Profit	£ 9,800.00	£ 9,500.00	£ 9,320.00	£ 28,620.00			
14	Cumulative	£ 9,800.00	£ 19,300.00	£ 28,620.00				
15								

Finally, use the **File, Save As** command to save your work under the filename **Project 3**.

Printing a Worksheet

To print a worksheet, make sure that the printer you propose to use was defined when you first installed Windows.

If you have named more than one printer in your original installation of Windows, and want to select a printer other than your original first choice, then select the **File, Print** (or <Ctrl+P>) command, click the down-arrow against the **Name** box on the displayed Print dialogue box and select the required printer, as shown below.

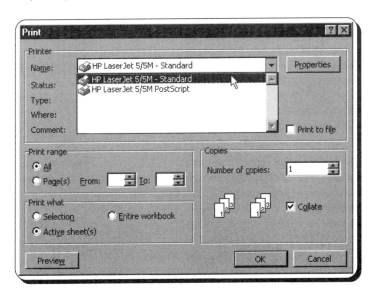

If you want to change the paper size, print orientation or printer resolution, click the **Properties** button on the Print dialogue box. These and other changes to the appearance of the printout can also be made by choosing the **File, Page Setup** command which causes the Page Setup dialogue box to be displayed, as shown overleaf.

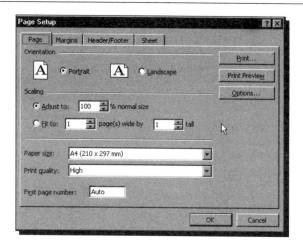

By selecting the appropriate Tab on this dialogue box, you can change your **Page** settings, page **Margins**, specify a **Header/Footer**, and control how a **Sheet** should be printed. Each Tab displays a different dialogue box, appropriate to the function at hand. In the **Header/Footer** dialogue box you can even click the down-arrow against the Header and Footer boxes to display a suggested list for these, appropriate to the work you are doing, the person responsible for it and even the date it is being carried out! Try it.

A very useful feature of Excel is the **Scaling** facility shown in the above dialogue box. You can print actual size or a percentage of it, or you can choose to fit your worksheet on to one page which allows Excel to scale your work automatically.

To preview a worksheet, click the 'Print Preview' icon on the Standard Toolbar, shown here, or click the **Print Preview** button on the Page Setup dialogue box, or the **Preview** button on the Print dialogue box. You can even use the **File, Print Preview** command!

The idea of all these preview choices is to make it easy for you to see your work on screen before committing it to paper, thus saving a few more trees!

Enhancing a Worksheet

You can make your work look more professional by adopting various enhancements, such as single and double line cell borders, shading certain cells, and adding meaningful headers and footers.

However, with Excel you can easily select a predefined style to display your work on both the screen and on paper. To do this, place the active cell within the table (or range) you want to format, say C5, then select the **Format, AutoFormat** command which will cause the following dialogue box to appear on the screen, displaying a sample of the chosen table format. In this way you can choose what best suits your needs. We selected 'Classic 2' and pressed **OK**.

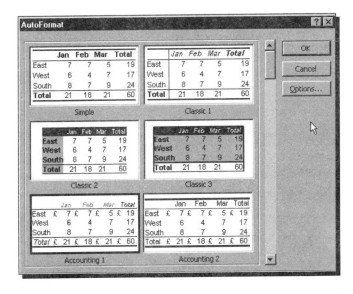

Next, reduce the title of the worksheet to 'Project Analysis', then centre it within the range A1:E1, by first selecting the range, then clicking the 'Merge and Centre' icon, shown here, which causes the title to centre within the specified range.

Finally, save the worksheet as **Project 4**, before going on.

Header and Footer Icons and Codes

Using the header and footer icons and their codes, shown below, you can position text or automatically insert information at the top or bottom of a report printout.

To add a header to our printed example, use the **File, Page Setup** command and click first the **Header/Footer** Tab, then the **Custom Header** button and type the information displayed below in the **Left section** and **Right section** of the Header box.

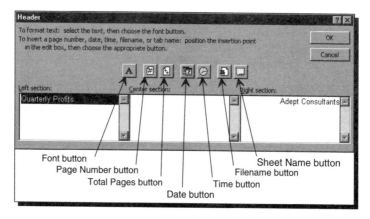

While the insertion pointer is in, say, the **Centre section** of the Header box, pointing and clicking on the 'Sheet Name' button, inserts the &[Tab] code which has the effect of inserting the sheet name of the current active sheet at the time of printing. The first icon button displays the Font dialogue box, while the others display the following codes:

Code	*Action*
&[Page]	Inserts a page number.
&[Pages]	Inserts the total number of pages.
&[Date]	Inserts the current date.
&[Time]	Inserts the current time.
&[File]	Inserts the filename of the current workbook.
&[Tab]	Inserts the name of the current sheet.

Setting a Print Area

To choose a smaller print area than the current worksheet, select the required area by highlighting the starting cell of the area and dragging the mouse, or using the **<Shift+Arrows>**, to highlight the block, and use the **File, Print** command which displays the following dialogue box:

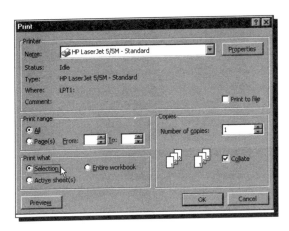

Choose the **Selection** button in the **Print What** box, and either click the **Preview** or the **OK** button to preview your report on screen or print it on paper. Once in preview mode, the following icons are available to you.

The first two allow you to change sheets, while the next one allows you to review your print output magnified or at full page size - when in full page size, the mouse pointer looks like a magnifying glass, as above. The next four icons can be used to print, change page settings, display and change the margins, or adjust the page size by dragging the page breaks to a new position. To return to normal view, click the **Close** button.

Another way to set the area to print is using the **File, Print Area, Set Print Area** menu command. To print selected sheets or the entire workbook, click the appropriate button in the **Print What** box of the Print dialogue box.

The default selection in the **Print What** box is **Active sheet(s)** which is also what will be printed out if you click the 'Print' icon, shown here. If you have included headers and footers, these will be printed out irrespective of whether you choose to print a selected range or a selected worksheet. To centre the page horizontally on the paper, use the **File, Page Setup** command, click the Margins tab and select the option. Finally, printing our worksheet, produces the following page:

Quarterly Profits	Sheet1	Adept Consultants

Project Analysis

	Jan	Feb	Mar	1st Quarter
Income	£ 14,000.00	£ 15,000.00	£ 16,000.00	£ 45,000.00
Costs:				
Wages	£ 2,000.00	£ 3,000.00	£ 4,000.00	£ 9,000.00
Travel	£ 400.00	£ 500.00	£ 600.00	£ 1,500.00
Rent	£ 300.00	£ 300.00	£ 300.00	£ 900.00
Heat/Light	£ 150.00	£ 200.00	£ 130.00	£ 480.00
Phone/Fax	£ 250.00	£ 300.00	£ 350.00	£ 900.00
Adverts	£ 1,100.00	£ 1,200.00	£ 1,300.00	£ 3,600.00
Total Costs	£ 4,200.00	£ 5,500.00	£ 6,680.00	£ 16,380.00
Profit	£ 9,800.00	£ 9,500.00	£ 9,320.00	£ 28,620.00
Cumulative	£ 9,800.00	£ 19,300.00	£ 28,620.00	

3-Dimensional Worksheets

In Excel, a Workbook is a 3-dimensional file made up with a series of flat 2-dimensional sheets stacked 'on top of each other'. Each sheet is the same size, and in itself, behaves the same as the more ordinary worksheets. As mentioned previously, each separate sheet in a file has its own Tab identifier at the bottom of the screen. Ranges can be set to span several different sheets to build up 3-dimensional blocks of data. These blocks can then be manipulated, copied, or moved to other locations in the file. A cell can reference any other cell in the file, no matter what sheet it is on, and an extended range of functions can be used to process these 3-dimensional ranges.

Manipulating Ranges

The best way to demonstrate a new idea is to work through an example - we will use the worksheet saved under 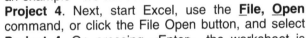 **Project 4**. Next, start Excel, use the **File, Open** command, or click the File Open button, and select **Project 4**. On pressing <Enter>, the worksheet is displayed on the screen as shown on the facing page.

Copying Sheets in a Workbook

We will now fill another three sheets behind the present one, in order to include information about ADEPT Consultants' trading during the other three quarters of the year. The easiest way of doing this is by copying the information in Sheet1, including the formatting and the entered formulae, onto the other three sheets, then edit the numerical information in these appropriately.

To simplify this operation, Excel has a facility which allows you to copy a sheet into a workbook. There are two ways of doing this: (a) with the mouse, or (b) using the menus.

With the mouse, make the sheet you want to copy the current sheet, then press the <Ctrl> key, and while keeping it pressed, point with the mouse on the Tab of Sheet1 and drag it to the right, as shown overleaf.

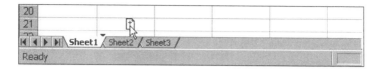

A small black triangle indicates the place where the copy will be inserted, as shown above. If you insert a copy, say before Sheet2, when you release the mouse button the inserted sheet will be given the name Sheet1(2), while inserting a second copy before Sheet2 will be given the name Sheet1(3).

To copy a sheet with the menus, select the **Edit, Move or Copy Sheet** command, then highlight Sheet2 in the **Before sheet** list of the displayed dialogue box, then check the **Create a copy** option at the bottom of the dialogue box, and press the **OK** button. Sheet1(2) will be inserted in the Workbook, in the above case.

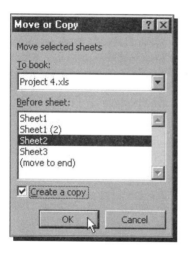

When you have three copies placed, double-click the Tabs of Sheet1 and the three new sheets and change their names to 'Quarter 1', 'Quarter 2', 'Quarter 3' and 'Quarter 4', respectively, as shown below.

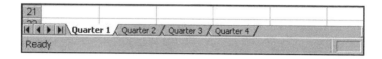

The contents of the second sheet should be as shown on the next page.

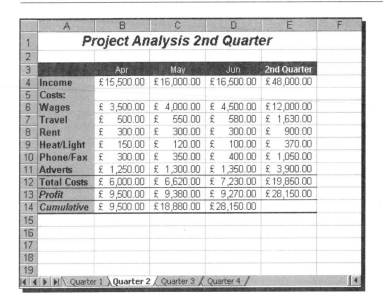

	A	B	C	D	E	F
1	*Project Analysis 2nd Quarter*					
2						
3		Apr	May	Jun	2nd Quarter	
4	Income	£ 15,500.00	£ 16,000.00	£ 16,500.00	£ 48,000.00	
5	Costs:					
6	Wages	£ 3,500.00	£ 4,000.00	£ 4,500.00	£ 12,000.00	
7	Travel	£ 500.00	£ 550.00	£ 580.00	£ 1,630.00	
8	Rent	£ 300.00	£ 300.00	£ 300.00	£ 900.00	
9	Heat/Light	£ 150.00	£ 120.00	£ 100.00	£ 370.00	
10	Phone/Fax	£ 300.00	£ 350.00	£ 400.00	£ 1,050.00	
11	Adverts	£ 1,250.00	£ 1,300.00	£ 1,350.00	£ 3,900.00	
12	Total Costs	£ 6,000.00	£ 6,620.00	£ 7,230.00	£ 19,850.00	
13	*Profit*	£ 9,500.00	£ 9,380.00	£ 9,270.00	£ 28,150.00	
14	*Cumulative*	£ 9,500.00	£ 18,880.00	£ 28,150.00		
15						
16						
17						
18						
19						

Quarter 1 \ **Quarter 2** / Quarter 3 / Quarter 4 /

The easiest way to enter these 2nd Quarter results is to edit the copied data (from Quarter 1) by either using the EDIT key (**F2**), or double-clicking the cell you want to edit. You should now be in a position to complete editing this sheet. Be extra careful, from now on, to check the identification Tab at the bottom of the screen, so as not to get the sheets mixed up. You do not want to spend time editing the wrong worksheet!

After building up the four worksheets (one for each quarter - see below for details on the 3rd and 4th quarters) save the file as **Project 5**.

	Jul	Aug	Sep	Oct	Nov	Dec
Income	17,000	17,500	18,000	18,500	19,000	19,500
Costs:						
Wages	4,000	4,500	5,000	4,500	5,000	5,500
Travel	600	650	680	630	670	700
Rent	300	300	300	300	300	300
Heat/Light	50	80	120	160	200	250
Phone/Fax	350	380	420	400	420	450
Adverts	1,400	1,450	1,500	1,480	1,500	1,530

Linking Sheets

A consolidation sheet could be placed in front of our 'stack' of data sheets to show a full year's results, by making a copy of the 1st Quarter sheet and placing it in front of it. Next, delete the entries in columns B to E, and name it 'Consolidation'.

We are now in a position to link the consolidation sheet to the other quarterly data sheets so that the information contained on them is automatically summarised and updated on it. The quarter totals in columns E of sheets Quarter 1, Quarter 2, Quarter 3, and Quarter 4, can be copied in turn to the clipboard using the **Edit, Copy** command, and then pasted to the appropriate column of the Consolidation sheet with the use of the **Edit, Paste Special** command and clicking the **Paste Link** button on the displayed dialogue box.

Note: Empty cells linked with this method, like those in cells E5 of each quarter, appear as 0 (zero) in the Consolidation sheet, and cannot be removed. To correct this, either copy each column E of each quarter in two stages; E3:E4, then E6:E13, or check the **Skip blanks** box in the Paste Special dialogue box. If you choose the latter method, you will have to increase the width of the relevant columns manually.

Next, insert appropriate formulae in row 14 to correctly calculate the cumulative values in the Consolidation sheet. The result should be as follows:

	A	B	C	D	E	F	G	H
1	*Project Analysis - Year Summary*							
2								
3		1st Quarter	2nd Quarter	3rd Quarter	4th Quarter			
4	Income	£ 45,000.00	£ 48,000.00	£ 52,500.00	£ 57,000.00			
5	Costs:							
6	Wages	£ 9,000.00	£ 12,000.00	£ 13,500.00	£ 15,000.00			
7	Travel	£ 1,500.00	£ 1,630.00	£ 1,930.00	£ 2,000.00			
8	Rent	£ 900.00	£ 900.00	£ 900.00	£ 900.00			
9	Heat/Light	£ 480.00	£ 370.00	£ 250.00	£ 610.00			
10	Phone/Fax	£ 900.00	£ 1,050.00	£ 1,150.00	£ 1,270.00			
11	Adverts	£ 3,600.00	£ 3,900.00	£ 4,350.00	£ 4,510.00			
12	Total Costs	£ 16,380.00	£ 19,850.00	£ 22,080.00	£ 24,290.00			
13	*Profit*	£ 28,620.00	£ 28,150.00	£ 30,420.00	£ 32,710.00			
14	*Cumulative*	£ 28,620.00	£ 56,770.00	£ 87,190.00	£ 119,900.00			
15								

Finally, save the resultant workbook as **Project 6**.

Linking Files

In the last example we built a consolidation report on a separate sheet in front of several parallel data sheets. All these sheets were, however, part of the same file. There may be times, however, when the consolidation data would be preferable in a separate file. As an example of linking files, we will work through an exercise to carry out this operation.

File Commands

Use the **File, Close** command to close **Project 6** and clear the computer's memory, and **File, Open** to open **Project 5**. Next, place another empty file in memory using the **File, New** command. You can tell that a new file has been created, because the filename Book2 appears on the Title bar.

We would like to paste links between columns E of each quarter sheet of file **Project 5** and the newly opened file. This is best done if both files can be viewed at the same time, so use the **Window, Arrange, Tiled** command, then copy all the labels from sheet Quarter 1 of the file **Project 5** onto Sheet1 of the new file using the **Edit, Copy** and **Edit, Paste Special** command. The result so far should be as follows:

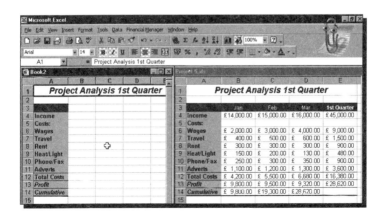

Note that in this version of Excel, the widths of columns containing labels have transferred across when copying in this manner and the heading in the first row is centred correctly. However, the widths of columns containing numbers do not transfer across. Therefore, adjust columns B to E to a width of 11.

Copying between files is the same as copying between the separate sheets of a file. However, here we would like to paste both the formats of the cells, and the links, therefore a two-fold copy and paste process is necessary. First, select in turn each quarter's totals from **Project 5** (cells E3:E14 of each sheet), use the **Edit, Copy** command, and paste the formats with the **Edit, Paste Special** command, clicking the **Formats** button on the displayed dialogue box, and pressing **OK**.

Next, select each contiguous part of each quarter separately (to avoid pasting zeros where spaces should appear), copy them, and paste them with file links onto Sheet1 of the new file in columns B to E, using the **Edit, Paste Special** command and pressing the **Paste Link** button on the displayed dialogue box. Below we show this process in action when the second quarter has just been linked to Sheet1 of Book2, but with the Paste Special dialogue box also open.

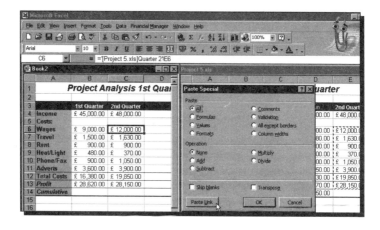

Below we show the maximised consolidated file for all four quarters, after changing the contents of cell A1 from 'Project Analysis 1st Quarter' to 'Project Analysis - Year Summary', and saving the linked books as **Adept 1**.

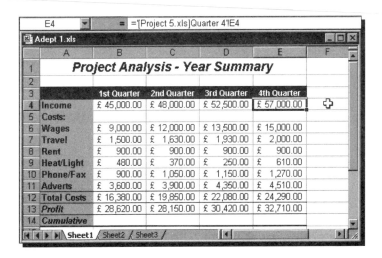

Note how cell references between different files (which could have been typed in) are shown with the filename and sheet name included in single quotes ('...'), placed before the cell address, if the sheet name includes a space. For example

='[Project 5.xls]Quarter 4'!E4

which implies that both files are on the same drive and path. However, once such a file is re-opened, the full reference to drive and path is given - see the screen dump on page 74 where the above formula is given as:

='D:\My Documents\WorkBooks\[Project 5.xls]Quarter 4'!E4

Next, add the appropriate formulae in row 14 to calculate the cumulative profits, and change the width of column E to 11.5 to accommodate the rather large year's end cumulative value.

Relative and Absolute Cell Addresses

Entering a mathematical expression into Excel, such as the formula in cell C14 which was

=B14+C13

causes Excel to interpret it as 'add the contents of cell one column to the left of the current position, to the contents of cell one row above the current position'. In this way, when the formula was later copied into cell address D14, the contents of the cell relative to the left position of D14 (i.e. C14) and the contents of the cell one row above it (i.e. D13) were used, instead of the original cell addresses entered in C14. This is relative addressing.

To see the effect of relative versus absolute addressing, copy the formula in cell C14 into C17, as shown below:

C17	▼	=	=B17+C16		
	A	B	C	D	E	F
1	*Project Analysis - Year Summary*					
2						
3		**1st Quarter**	2nd Quarter	3rd Quarter	**4th Quarter**	
4	**Income**	£ 45,000.00	£ 48,000.00	£ 52,500.00	£ 57,000.00	
5	**Costs:**					
6	**Wages**	£ 9,000.00	£ 12,000.00	£ 13,500.00	£ 15,000.00	
7	**Travel**	£ 1,500.00	£ 1,630.00	£ 1,930.00	£ 2,000.00	
8	**Rent**	£ 900.00	£ 900.00	£ 900.00	£ 900.00	
9	**Heat/Light**	£ 480.00	£ 370.00	£ 250.00	£ 610.00	
10	**Phone/Fax**	£ 900.00	£ 1,050.00	£ 1,150.00	£ 1,270.00	
11	**Adverts**	£ 3,600.00	£ 3,900.00	£ 4,350.00	£ 4,510.00	
12	**Total Costs**	£ 16,380.00	£ 19,850.00	£ 22,080.00	£ 24,290.00	
13	*Profit*	£ 28,620.00	£ 28,150.00	£ 30,420.00	£ 32,710.00	
14	*Cumulative*	£ 28,620.00	£ 56,770.00	£ 87,190.00	£ 119,900.00	
15						
16						
17			£ -	⊕		

Note that in cell C14 the formula was =B14+C13. However, when copied into cell C17 the formula appears as

=B17+C16

This is because it has been interpreted as relative addressing. In this case, no value appears in cell C17 because we are attempting to add two blank cells.

Now change the formula in C14 by editing it to

=$B$14+$C$13

which is interpreted as absolute addressing. Copying this formula into cell C17 calculates the correct result. Highlight cell C17 and observe the cell references in its formula; they have not changed from those of cell C14.

The $ sign must prefix both the column reference and the row reference. Mixed cell addressing is permitted; as for example when a column address reference is needed to be taken as absolute, while a row address reference is needed to be taken as relative. In such a case, the column letter is prefixed by the $ sign.

When building an absolute cell reference in a formula, it is easier to select each cell address within a formula by double-clicking on it with the left mouse button then, when selected, keep on pressing the **F4** key until the correct $ prefix is set.

Freezing Panes on Screen

Sometimes there might be too much information on screen and attempting to see a certain part of a sheet might cause the labels associated with that information to scroll off the screen.

To freeze column (or row) labels of a worksheet on screen, move the cell pointer to the right (or below) the column (or row) which you want to freeze, and use the **Window, Freeze Panes** command. Everything to the left of (or above) the cell pointer will freeze on the screen.

In the example on the next page, the cell pointer was placed in cell B4 of the **Adept 1** workbook, before issuing the command to freeze the panes.

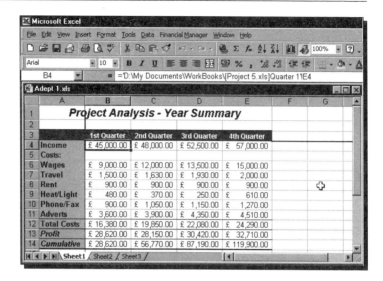

As seen on the screen dump above, Excel added a vertical line between columns A and B, and a horizontal line between rows 3 and 4. Scrolling horizontally or vertically leaves column A and rows 1-3 always on the screen.

To remove unwanted frozen panes, or move their position on the worksheet, use the **Window, Unfreeze Panes** command.

5

Spreadsheet Charts

Excel allows information within a worksheet to be represented in graphical form, which makes data more accessible to non-expert users who might not be familiar with the spreadsheet format. The saying 'a picture is worth a thousand words', applies equally well to charts and figures.

The package includes several chart and graph types, such as area, bar, column, line, doughnut, radar, XY, pie, combination, and several 3-D options of these charts. In all, Excel allows fourteen different types of charts, with almost 100 predefined formats, which can be selected by using the appropriate icon. These are made available to you once you have selected the data you want to chart and clicked on the Chart Wizard button on the toolbar.

Charts (you can have several per worksheet) can be displayed on screen at the same time as the worksheet from which they were derived, since they appear in their own 'chart' frame and can be embedded anywhere on a worksheet. Furthermore, they can be sent to an appropriate output device, such as a plotter or printer. Although this charting module rivals a standalone graphics package, and one could write a separate book on it, an attempt will be made to present its basics, in the space available within this book.

Preparing for a Column Chart

In order to illustrate some of the graphing capabilities of Excel, we will now plot the income of the consulting company we discussed in the **Project 6** file. However, before we can go on, you will need to complete the entries for the last two quarters of trading of the Adept Consultants' example, if you haven't already done so - see end of previous chapter.

Next, link the quarterly totals to the consolidation sheet, calculate the year's total, as shown below, and save the resultant workbook as **Project 7**, before going on.

	F4	▼		=	=SUM(B4:E4)	
	A	B	C	D	E	F	G
1	*Project Analysis - Year Summary*						
2							
3		1st Quarter	2nd Quarter	3rd Quarter	4th Quarter	Total	
4	Income	£45,000.00	£48,000.00	£52,500.00	£ 57,000.00	£202,500.00	
5	Costs:						
6	Wages	£ 9,000.00	£12,000.00	£13,500.00	£ 15,000.00	£ 49,500.00	
7	Travel	£ 1,500.00	£ 1,630.00	£ 1,930.00	£ 2,000.00	£ 7,060.00	
8	Rent	£ 900.00	£ 900.00	£ 900.00	£ 900.00	£ 3,600.00	
9	Heat/Light	£ 480.00	£ 370.00	£ 250.00	£ 610.00	£ 1,710.00	
10	Phone/Fax	£ 900.00	£ 1,050.00	£ 1,150.00	£ 1,270.00	£ 4,370.00	
11	Adverts	£ 3,600.00	£ 3,900.00	£ 4,350.00	£ 4,510.00	£ 16,360.00	
12	Total Costs	£16,380.00	£19,850.00	£22,080.00	£ 24,290.00	£ 82,600.00	
13	*Profit*	£28,620.00	£28,150.00	£30,420.00	£ 32,710.00	£119,900.00	
14	*Cumulative*	£28,620.00	£56,770.00	£87,190.00	£ 119,900.00		
15							

Now we need to select the range of the data we want to graph. The range of data to be graphed in Excel does not have to be contiguous for each graph, as with some other spreadsheets. With Excel, you select your data from different parts of a sheet with the <Ctrl> key pressed down. This method has the advantage of automatic recalculation should any changes be made to the original data. You could also collect data from different sheets to one 'graphing' sheet by linking them as we did with the consolidation sheet.

If you don't want the chart to be recalculated when you do this, then you must use the **Edit, Copy** and **Edit, Paste Special** commands and choose the **Values** option from the displayed dialogue box, which copies a selected range to a specified target area of the worksheet and converts formulae to values. This is necessary, as cells containing formulae cannot be pasted directly since it would cause the relative cell addresses to adjust to the new locations; each formula would then recalculate a new value for each cell and give wrong results.

The Chart Wizard

To obtain a chart of 'Income' versus 'Quarters', select the data in cell range A3..E4, then either click the Chart Wizard button, shown here, or use the **Insert, Chart** command. The Chart Wizard then opens the first of four dialogue boxes, as shown below, which guide you through the process.

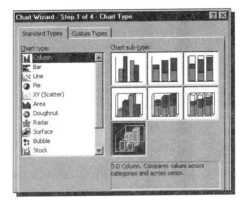

Now select the 3-D Column type and click the **Next >** button at the bottom of the displayed Chart Wizard dialogue box (not shown above). The second dialogue box is then displayed, and looks similar to the one below, provided you click the **Co_umns** radio button.

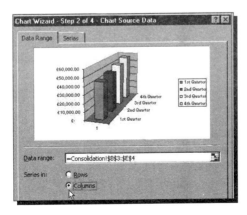

The third Chart Wizard dialogue box allows you to give a title to your chart and annotate the x- and y-axes, while the fourth dialogue box allows you to place the chart either on a separate sheet or on the sheet that was active when you first started the charting process. When you press the **Finish** button the following chart should appear on your worksheet.

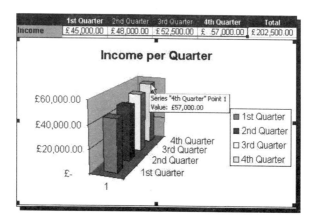

Note that to find out the exact details of a given column on a chart, you need only place the mouse pointer on it to cause a banner to appear with the desired information.

While the frame containing a chart is selected (you can tell from the presence of the small black squares around it), you can change its size by dragging the small two-headed arrow pointer (which appears when the mouse pointer is placed on the small black squares of the frame). You can also move the frame and its contents to another position on the worksheet by pointing to the chart area, pressing and keeping depressed the left mouse button until the pointer changes to a small four-headed arrow shape, then dragging the changed mouse pointer to a new position.

As an example of what you can do with a chart, let us first select it, then either double-click within the chart area or use the **Format, Selected Chart Area** command to obtain the following dialogue box:

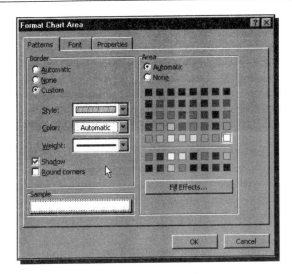

From this dialogue box you can choose a pattern to be used as a frame, by selecting **Custom** under the Patterns tab and choose the 8th <u>S</u>**tyle**, the 4th <u>W</u>**eight** line, check the Sha<u>d</u>**ow** box and press **OK**.

Try it, then change the second quarter income from £48,000 to £58,000 (on the Quarter 2 sheet), and watch how the change is reflected on the redrawn graph on the Consolidation sheet displayed below.

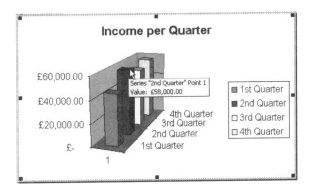

You can change the type of chart shown on screen by first selecting it, then using the **Chart, Chart Type** command to display the first Chart Wizard dialogue box.

Finally, revert to the original entry for the first quarter's income, change your chart back to a simple column type, and then save your work again under the filename **Project 7** by simply pressing the Save icon shown here. Your current work will be saved to disc replacing the previous version under the same filename.

When Excel creates a chart, it plots each row or column of data in the selected range as a 'data series', such as a group of bars, lines, etc. A chart can contain many data series, but Excel charts data according to the following rules:

1.   If the selected range contains more rows than columns of data, Excel plots the data series by columns.

X-axis labels   1st data series   2nd data series   3rd data series

2.   If the selected range contains more columns than rows of data, or the same number of columns and rows, Excel plots the data series by rows.

If you select a range to chart which includes column and row headings, and text above or to the left of the numeric data, Excel uses the text to create the axis labels, legends, and title.

If your data selection does not obey these rules, you must tell Excel how your data series is structured in the 2nd Chart Wizard dialogue box.

Editing a Chart

The easiest way to edit a chart is to right-click it while pointing within the chart area, but near its outer rim. This displays the shortcut menu shown here. As a chart is made up of several objects, for example, data series, plot area, the various axis data area, legends, and chart area, you will get a different shortcut menu if you were pointing to these different areas. Try it. As you right-click different areas, their name will appear in the 'Name box' which is situated below the 'Font' box. The shortcut menu shown here is the one you will get when you right-click the 'Chart Area'.

We have already used the first menu option to format our chart. The second menu option allows you to quickly change the chart type, while the third option can be used to change the source data. The fourth menu option allows you to add Titles, change axes, add grid lines and data labels, while the fifth option lets you specify whether you want your chart to be located in a new sheet or where you created it.

Saving Charts

When you save a workbook, the chart or charts you have created are saved with it. It is, therefore, a good idea not only to give each chart a title, but to also locate it on a differently named sheet.

Use the **Chart Options** in the above shortcut menu to give this chart the title **Income per Quarter**, and the **Location** option to put the chart on a separate sheet and give it the name **Income Bar**. Finally, save the workbook under the filename **Project 8**.

Pre-defined Chart Types

To select a different type of chart, click the Chart Wizard icon shown here, or select the **Insert, Chart** command. The 1st Chart Wizard dialogue box displayed previously, lists 14 different chart options. These chart-types are normally used to describe the following relationships between data:

	Area:	for showing a volume relationship between two series, such as production or sales, over a given length of time.
	Bar:	for comparing differences in data (noncontinuous data that are not related over time) by depicting changes in horizontal bars to show positive and negative variations from a given position.
	Bubble:	for showing a type of XY (scatter) chart. The size of the data (radius of the bubble) indicates the value of a third variable.
	Column:	for comparing separate items (noncontinuous data which are related over time) by depicting changes in vertical bars to show positive and negative variations from a given position.
	Cone:	for showing 3-D column and bar charts in a more dramatic way.
	Cylinder:	similar to Cone.
	Doughnut:	for comparing parts with the whole. Similar to pie charts, but can depict more than one series of data.

Line: for showing continuous changes in data with time.

Pie: for comparing parts with the whole. You can use this type of chart when you want to compare the percentage of an item from a single series of data with the whole series.

Pyramid: similar to Cone.

Radar: for plotting one series of data as angle values defined in radians, against one or more series defined in terms of a radius.

Surface: for showing optimum combinations between two sets of data, as in a topographic map. Colours and patterns indicate areas that are in the same range of values.

Stock: for showing high-low-close type of data variation to illustrate stock market prices or temperature changes.

XY (Scatter): for showing scatter relationships between X and Y. Scatter charts are used to depict items which are not related over time.

You can change the type of chart by selecting one of the fourteen offered when the **Chart Type** button is clicked on the Chart Toolbar. This bar is opened whenever a chart is selected, as follows,

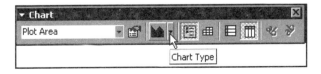

provided you have activated it using the **View**, **Toolbars** command.

Customising a Chart

In order to customise a chart, you need to know how to add legends, titles, text labels, arrows, and how to change the colour and pattern of the chart background, plot areas and chart markers, and how to select, move and size chart objects.

Drawing a Multiple Column Chart

As an exercise, we will consider a new column chart which deals with the quarterly 'Costs' of Adept Consultants. To achieve this, first select the Consolidation sheet of workbook **Project 8**, then highlight the cell range A3:E3, press the <Ctrl> key, and while holding it down, use the mouse to select the costs range A6:E11.

Next, click the Chart Wizard icon (or use the **Insert, Chart** command), select Column from the **Chart type** list, click the fourth **Chart subtype** option, and press the **Next** button. The 6 different quarterly costs will be drawn automatically, as displayed in the composite screen dump below.

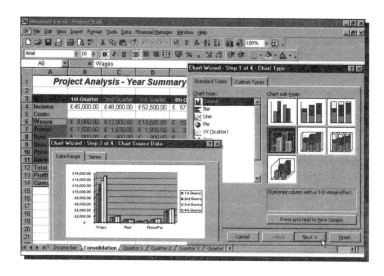

Because the selected range contains more rows than columns of data, Excel follows the 1st rule of data series selection which, however, might not be what you want.

To have the 'quarters' appearing on the x-axis and the 'costs' as the legends, we need to tell Excel that our data series is in rows by clicking the **Rows** button on the 2nd Chart Wizard dialogue box. Immediately this is done the column chart changes to:

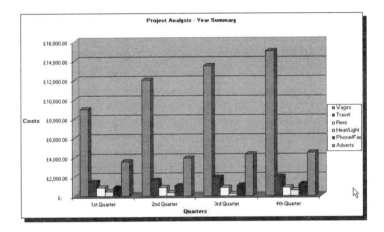

The chart title and axes titles were inserted by typing the heading 'PROJECT ANALYSIS - Year Summary' in the **Chart title** box of the 3rd Chart Wizard dialogue box, followed by the **Axis Titles** shown above.

Once you are satisfied with your efforts, click the **As new sheet** radio button of the 4th Chart Wizard dialogue box, and name your chart **Costs Bar**. If you make a mistake and you want to try again, make sure the unwanted chart is selected, then press the <Del> key. Finally, save your work under the filename **Project 9**.

Changing a Title and an Axis Label

To change a title, an axis label, or a legend within a chart, click the appropriate area on the chart. This reveals that these are individual objects (they are surrounded by small black squares) and you can edit, reposition them, or change their font and point size. You can even rotate text within such areas in any direction you like.

To demonstrate these options, we will use the **Costs Bar** chart saved in **Project 9**, so get it on screen if you are to follow our suggestions.

To change the font size of a chart title, click the Chart Title area to select it and double-click on the border that is displayed when you select such an object. Doing this, displays the Format dialogue box for the selected object, and clicking the Font tab reveals the following:

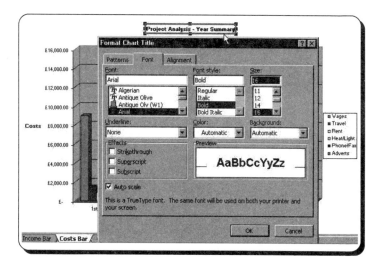

From here, we changed the font size of the chart title from 12 to 16 points. We also selected the Costs label and changed its size from 10 to 14 points, then clicked the Alignment tab to change its orientation to 90°, as shown on the next page.

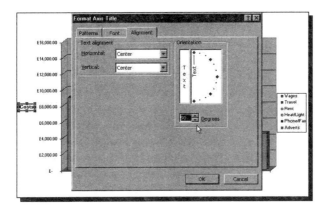

Drawing a Pie Chart

To change the chart type, simply select the chart, then click the Chart Wizard and choose the 3-D Pie chart from the displayed list. If the selected chart was the 'quarterly costs' chart, then clicking the **Next** button, checking the **Columns** radio button and clicking **Next**, displays the chart type that would be redrawn for the specified data series, as shown below.

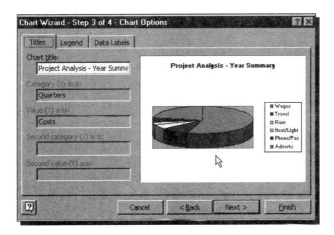

However, so as not to spoil your **Costs Bar** chart, click the **Cancel** button at this stage.

To obtain a pie chart without spoiling the chart it is based on, you must select the data range again, then click the Chart Wizard, choose the pie chart from the displayed chart types, then select the specific pie chart that best fits your data, specify the type of series, and give the chart a title.

As a last example in chart drawing, we will use the data range A6:A11 and F6:F11 of the Consolidation worksheet to plot a 3-D pie chart. The steps are the same as before, but for the 3-D option and specifying the type of series data as 'columns'. Note that the chart title should now reflect the Year Totals, rather than the Quarter summaries. The result should be as follows:

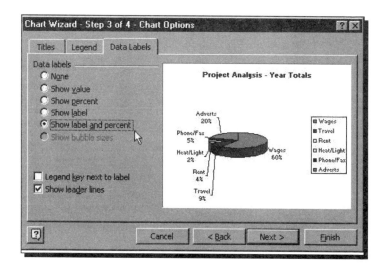

To display the above chart, we clicked the Data Labels tab and the **Show label and percent** radio button in the 3rd dialogue box of the Chart Wizard.

This chart tells us, for example, that Wages for the whole year amount to 60% of the total yearly costs. Other cost categories are also displayed with their appropriate percentages. Clicking the **Finish** button displays the pie chart in its finished form, as shown overleaf.

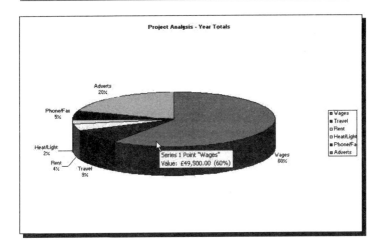

Pointing to any pie slice, causes the pop-up poster to be displayed, informing you of the actual data series, its value and its percentage of the whole. It is now obvious that the information contained in this chart is much more than in the 2-D version.

If you want to explode an individual pie slice, you can do so by simply dragging it. This is possible as each slice is treated as a separate object, but you must increase the size of your chart before you can accurately pinpoint the required slice.

Finally, use the **Chart, Location** menu command to name this last version of the pie chart as **Costs Pie** and save your workbook.

The Drawing Tools

Should you want to create a drawing in your document, use the **View, Toolbars** command and select **Drawing** from the drop-down menu. You can use the Drawing tools to create, or edit, a graphic consisting of lines, arcs, ellipses, rectangles, and even text boxes. These can either exist in their own right, or be additions to a picture or object.

The various buttons on the Drawing toolbar have the following functions (see also next page):

Group objects, etc.

Select Objects

Free Rotate

Select from various shapes

Line

Arrow

Rectangle

Oval

Text Box

Insert WordArt

Insert Clip Art

Fill Colour

Shadow

3-D

More Buttons

The Drawing Toolbar

The various functions offered by the Drawing Toolbar are shared by all Office 2000 applications and give Excel a superior graphics capability. Amongst the many features available are:

AutoShapes – the additional AutoShape categories, such as connectors, block arrows, flowchart symbols, stars and banners, callouts, and action buttons make drawing diagrams much easier.

Bezier curves – used to easily create exact curves with pinpoint precision.

3-D effects – allow you to transform 2-D shapes into realistic 3-D objects with new 3-D effects, such as changing the lighting perspective of a 3-D object.

Perspective shadows – allow you to select from a wide range of shadows with perspective, and you can adjust the depth and angle of each shadow to make pictures more realistic.

Connectors – used to create diagrams and flowcharts with new straight, angled, and curved connectors between the shapes; when shapes are moved, the connectors remain attached and automatically reposition themselves.

Arrowhead styles – allow you to change the width and height of arrowheads for maximum effect.

Object alignment – allow you to distribute and space objects evenly, both horizontally and vertically.

Precise line-width control – allows you increased control over the width of lines by selecting pre-set options or customised line widths.

Image editing – lets you easily adjust the brightness or contrast of a picture.

Transparent background – allows you to insert a bit map on your slides or Web pages so as to appear to be part of the design by turning background colours into transparent areas.

Creating a Drawing

The effects of the drawing tools can be superimposed either on the worksheet area or on top of a chart. The result is that you should be able to annotate worksheets and charts to your total satisfaction.

To create an object, click on the required Drawing button, such as the **Oval** or **Rectangle**, position the mouse pointer where you want to create the object on the screen, and then drag the mouse to draw the object. Hold the <Shift> key while you drag the mouse to create a perfect circle or square. If you do not hold <Shift>, Excel creates an oval or a rectangle.

You can use the **AutoShapes** button to select from a variety of pre-drawn **Lines**, **Basic Shapes**, etc. First click on the desired line or shape, then position the mouse pointer where you want to create the object on the screen and click the left mouse button to fix it on that position.

Editing a Drawing

To select an object, click on it. Excel displays white handles around the object selected.

You can move an object, or multiple objects, within a draw area by selecting them and dragging to the desired position. To copy an object, click at the object, then use the **Edit, Copy** / **Edit, Paste** commands.

To size an object, position the mouse pointer on a white handle and then drag the handle until the object is the desired shape and size.

To delete an object, select it and press the <Del> key. To delete a drawing, hold the <Shift> key down and click each object in turn that makes up the drawing, unless they are grouped or framed, then press <Del>.

Do try out some of these commands using the **Project 9** workbook file. For example, try drawing an arrow to point to the largest expenditure and label it appropriately, but if you make any mistakes, do not save the results of your experimentation under the same file name.

6

The Excel Database

An Excel database table is a worksheet range which contains related information, such as 'Customer's Names', 'Consultancy Details', 'Invoice No.', etc. A phone book is a simple database table, stored on paper. In Excel each record is entered as a worksheet row, with the fields of each record occupying corresponding columns.

A database table is a collection of data that exists, and is organised around a specific theme or requirement. It is used for storing information so that it is quickly accessible. To make accessing the data easier, each row (or **record)**, of data within a database table is structured in the same fashion, i.e. each record will have the same number of columns (or **fields**).

We define a database and its various elements as follows:

Database table	A collection of related data organised in rows and columns in a worksheet file. A worksheet file can contain many different database tables.
Record	A row of information relating to a single entry and comprising one or more fields.
Field	A single column of information of the same type, such as people's names.

In Excel 2000, a database table can contain a maximum of 256 fields and 65,536 records. Furthermore, you can have up to 32,000 characters in a cell. These specifications were first introduced in the 97 version of the program.

Creating a Database

In order to investigate the various database functions, such as sorting, searching, etc., we first need to set up a database table in the form shown on the next page.

Note that in creating a database table, the following rules must be observed:

1. The top row of the database table must contain the field labels, one per column, which identify the fields in the database table. The second and subsequent rows of such a database table must contain records; no blank rows should be inserted between the field labels and the records.

2. Field labels must be unique within a given database table.

3. Entries under each field must be of the same type.

4. The size of a database table must be limited within the design criteria of the package (256 fields and 65,536 records).

We assume that the 'Invoice Analysis' of Adept Consultants is designed and set out as shown below with the listed field titles and field widths.

Column	Title	Width	Type
A	NAME	21	General or Text
B	DETAILS	20	General or Text
C	No.	6	Number, 0 decimals
D	ISSUED	9	Custom, dd/mm/yy
E	PAID?	7	General or Text
F	VALUE	8	Currency, 2 decimals

These widths were chosen so that the whole worksheet could be seen on the screen at once.

If you cannot see all the rows of this database on your screen at once (it depends on the configuration of your display under Windows - see below), either select the **View, Zoom** command and set the zoom level to say 90%, or toggle off the **Drawing** and/or **Status Toolbars**.

If, on the other hand, you did not want to change your Excel configuration, but prefer to change the configuration of your display, then click the **Start** button and select **Settings, Control Panel**, double-click the Display icon and click the Setting tab of the Display Properties dialogue box. In our case, the **Screen area** was set to 800 by 600 pixels and the **Font size** (use the **Advance** button) to Small. However, do remember that if you carry out these changes, they will not take effect until you restart Windows.

	A	B	C	D	E	F	G
1		INVOICE ANALYSIS: ADEPT CONSULTANTS LTD AT					23/10/99
2							
3	NAME	DETAILS	No.	ISSUED	PAID?	VALUE	
4	VORTEX Co. Ltd	Wind Tunnel Tests	99001	10/04/99	N	£120.84	
5	AVON Construction	Adhesive Tests	99002	14/04/99	Y	£103.52	
6	BARROWS Associates	Tunnel Design Tests	99003	20/04/99	N	£99.32	
7	STONEAGE Ltd	Carbon Dating Tests	99004	05/05/99	N	£55.98	
8	PARKWAY Gravel	Material Size Tests (XX)	99005	11/05/99	N	£180.22	
9	WESTWOOD Ltd	Load Bearing Tests	99006	25/05/99	N	£68.52	
10	GLOWORM Ltd	Luminescence Tests	99007	10/06/99	N	£111.55	
11	SILVERSMITH Co	X-Ray Diffraction Test	99008	20/06/99	Y	£123.45	
12	WORMGLAZE Ltd	Heat Transfer Tests	99009	30/06/99	N	£35.87	
13	EALING Engines Design	Vibration Tests	99010	05/07/99	N	£58.95	
14	HIRE Service Equipment	Network Implementation	99011	15/07/99	N	£290.00	
15	EUROBASE Co. Ltd	Project Control	99012	22/07/99	N	£150.00	
16	FREEMARKET Dealers	Stock Control Package	99013	03/08/99	N	£560.00	
17	OILRIG Construct.	Metal Fatigue Tests	99014	12/08/99	N	£96.63	
18	TIME & Motion Ltd	Systems Analysis	99015	26/08/99	N	£120.35	
19	AVON Construction	Cement Fatigue Tests	99016	07/09/99	N	£111.89	
20	PARKWAY Gravel	Material Size Tests (ZZ)	99017	15/09/99	N	£190.35	

To change the width of the various columns to those given on the previous page, use the **Format, Column, Width** command (or use the mouse to drag the vertical separators of the column borders). Next, enter the abbreviated titles, centrally positioned, in row 3, as shown in the worksheet above.

The formatting type was selected by using the **F<u>o</u>rmat, C<u>e</u>lls** command to display the dialogue box below.

This dialogue box was used to format column C to a **Number** category format (with 0 decimal places), column D to a **Custom** category format (type dd/mm/yy), and column F to a **Currency** format (with 2 decimal places).

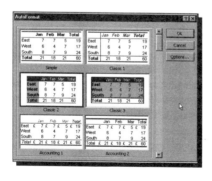

Finally, enter the numeric information in your worksheet and save the worksheet under the filename **Invoice 1**. You could format your database further by choosing a design from a list in the AutoFormat dialogue box, as shown here, prior to saving your work. However, we leave this to you, as it is entirely a matter of personal choice.

Sorting a Database List

The records within our database list are in the order in which they were entered, with the 'Invoice No' shown in ascending order. However, we might find it easier to browse through the information if it was sorted in alphabetical order of 'Customer's Name'. Excel has an easy way to do this.

To use it, highlight the database list (data range A4:F20; don't include the field names in the range to be sorted) and, either press the 'Sort Ascending' button, shown to the left, or select the **Data, Sort** command, and choose in the **Sort By** list of the Sort dialogue box the name of the field on which you want to sort the database (in this case NAME). This will be the primary sort key.

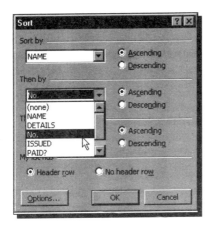

This second method of sorting allows you more control over the sorting options, such as the choice of a secondary sort key (in this case No.). This is selected in the **Then by** list of the Sort dialogue box, shown above, which ensures that the lowest number invoices appear first, if a company has been issued with more than one invoice. You even have the choice of a third sort key, if you needed one.

Pressing the **OK** button produces the display shown on the next page.

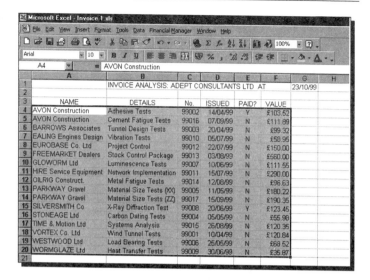

The easiest way to return the database to its original sort order is by selecting the **Edit, Undo Sort** command or you can re-sort the database in ascending order of Invoice No.

Date Arithmetic

There are several date functions which can be used in Excel to carry out date calculations. For example, typing the function =DATE(99,10,23) returns the date 23/10/99. The function =DATEVALUE("23/10/99"), returns the date 23/10/99 provided the cell is formatted as a **Custom** category (type dd/mm/yy), otherwise if the cell was formatted as **General**, or **Number**, then Excel would return the number of days since 1 January 1900.

Typing the function =NOW( ), returns the current date and time as given by your computer's internal clock. The cell is formatted automatically as **Custom** (type dd/mm/yy hh.mm). If the cell was formatted as **Number**, then Excel would have returned a decimal number representing the number of days since 1 January 1900, with the digits after the decimal point representing a fraction of a day.

With Excel 2000 you don't need to use the DATE and DATEVALUE functions when entering dates. You could, for example, write in a cell the formula:

=NOW()–D4

which allows Excel to calculate the difference in days between now and the mentioned date, provided the cell was formatted as **Number**. We could use this formula to work out the number of overdue days of the unpaid invoices in our example, by typing it in cell G4. However, if you want to compare the numbers you get with those displayed in this book, use instead the following formula:

=$G$1–D4

where $G$1 causes an 'absolute' reference to be made to the contents of cell G1. If the record in row 4 of the worksheet refers to the data of VORTEX Co. Ltd., then the result should be 196 days.

However, before we proceed to copy the above formula to the rest of the G column of the database list, we should take into consideration the fact that, normally, such information is not necessary if an invoice has been paid. Therefore, we need to edit the above formula in such a way as to make the result conditional to non-payment of the issued invoice.

The IF Function

The IF function allows comparison between two values using special 'logical' operators. The logical operators we can use are listed below.

Logical	operators
=	Equal to
<	Less than
>	Greater than
<=	Less than or Equal to
>=	Greater than or Equal to
<>	Not Equal to

The general format of the IF function is as follows:

IF(Comparison,Outcome-if-true,Outcome-if-false)

which contains three arguments separated by commas.

The first argument of the IF function is the 'logical comparison', the second is what should happen if the outcome of the logical comparison is 'true', while the third is what should happen if the outcome of the logical comparison is 'false'.

Thus, we can incorporate the IF function in the formula we entered in cell G4 to calculate the days overdue only if the invoice has not been paid, otherwise the string 'N/A' should be written into the appropriate cell, should the contents of the corresponding E column of a record be anything else but N. Either edit the formula in cell G4, by double-clicking the cell, or retype it. The final version of the formula in cell G4 should now correspond to:

=IF(E4="N",$G$1–D4," N/A")

Now copy this formula to the rest of the appropriate range (G5:G20) and compare your results with those shown below.

	A	B	C	D	E	F	G
1	✥	INVOICE ANALYSIS: ADEPT CONSULTANTS LTD AT					23/10/99
2							
3	NAME	DETAILS	No.	ISSUED	PAID?	VALUE	OVERDUE
4	VORTEX Co. Ltd	Wind Tunnel Tests	99001	10/04/99	N	£120.84	196
5	AVON Construction	Adhesive Tests	99002	14/04/99	Y	£103.52	N/A
6	BARROWS Associates	Tunnel Design Tests	99003	20/04/99	N	£99.32	186
7	STONEAGE Ltd	Carbon Dating Tests	99004	05/05/99	N	£55.98	171
8	PARKWAY Gravel	Material Size Tests (XX)	99005	11/05/99	N	£180.22	165
9	WESTWOOD Ltd	Load Bearing Tests	99006	25/05/99	N	£68.52	151
10	GLOWORM Ltd	Luminescence Tests	99007	10/06/99	N	£111.55	135
11	SILVERSMITH Co	X-Ray Diffraction Test	99008	20/06/99	Y	£123.45	N/A
12	WORMGLAZE Ltd	Heat Transfer Tests	99009	30/06/99	N	£35.87	115
13	EALING Engines Design	Vibration Tests	99010	05/07/99	N	£58.95	110
14	HIRE Service Equipment	Network Implementation	99011	15/07/99	N	£290.00	100
15	EUROBASE Co. Ltd	Project Control	99012	22/07/99	N	£150.00	93
16	FREEMARKET Dealers	Stock Control Package	99013	03/08/99	N	£560.00	81
17	OILRIG Construct.	Metal Fatigue Tests	99014	12/08/99	N	£96.63	72
18	TIME & Motion Ltd	Systems Analysis	99015	26/08/99	N	£120.35	58
19	AVON Construction	Cement Fatigue Tests	99016	07/09/99	N	£111.89	46
20	PARKWAY Gravel	Material Size Tests (ZZ)	99017	15/09/99	N	£190.35	38

Your results might differ from the ones shown above, if you have used the NOW( ) function in cell G1. Check your work, then save it under the filename **Invoice 2**.

Searching a Database

A database can be searched for specific records that meet certain criteria. We will use the database of worksheet **Invoice 2** to illustrate the method.

Assuming that the database is on your screen, we need only place the cell pointer within the data list (we put it on cell A4, although anywhere within the range A4:G20 would do), for Excel to instinctively know the range of your data.

Using the Database Form

After the cell pointer is placed within the database list, Excel automatically creates a database form, as shown below, which is accessed by selecting the **Data, Form** command. The database form can be used to add, delete, edit, and search for specific records.

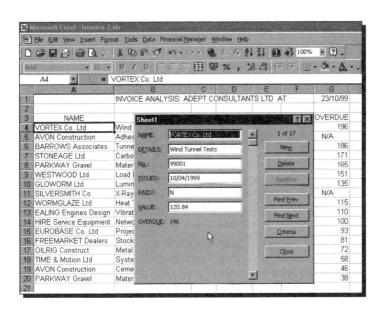

Note that the field names in the top row of the database appear on the left side of the form. On the top right corner of the form (above the **New** button) the entry '1 of 17' is displayed to indicate that this is the first of 17 records.

Most of the field names within the database form have one letter underlined, which can be used to access the corresponding box in the middle of the form in which the value of each field of the particular record is shown. To select fields or buttons, press the <Alt> key plus the underlined letter on field text or button, or point and click with the mouse. To move the focus forward through fields and buttons press the <Tab> key, while to move backwards, press <Shift+Tab>.

With the help of the database form, adding new records is made easy. On pressing the **New** button, an empty form is displayed for you to fill in. Editing a displayed record is even easier; that is why the **Restore** button is included. The functions of the form buttons are as follows:

Button	*Function*
New	Clears the field entries in the displayed form so that new information can be added. Pressing **New** again, adds the data just typed as a new record in the database.
Delete	Deletes the displayed record and shifts the remaining records one up the list. A deleted record cannot be restored. If you delete a record accidentally, re-open the database file without saving the changes.
Restore	Restores edited fields in the displayed record, removing the changes just made. Entries must be restored before pressing <Enter> to scroll to another record, or clicking the **Close** button.
Find Prev	Displays the previous record in the list. If criteria have been selected, then pressing **Find Prev** displays the previous record that matches the criteria.

Find Next   Displays the next record in the list. If criteria have been selected, then pressing **Find Next** displays the next record that matches the criteria.

Criteria   Displays a dialogue box in which you can enter comparison criteria with comparison operators to find records that meet these restrictions.

Close   Closes the data form.

Clear   Available after pressing the **Criteria** button. It removes existing criteria from the Criteria dialogue box.

Form   Available after pressing the **Criteria** button. It returns you to the default data form.

Finding Records

There are two ways of finding specific records from within a database. The first method involves the use of the database form, while the second method involves the filtering of data by using a criteria range within the worksheet to display only the rows that meet all the specified criteria.

Excel's database form can be used to find records provided the records we are looking for meet simple criteria. To enter the criteria, press the **Criteria** button on the database form which will cause a blank form to be displayed, with the cursor blinking in the first field. Now move the cursor to the 'PAID?' field and type N, then to the 'VALUE' field and type >150, as shown on the next page.

Pressing the **Find Next** button, displays the first record that meets both these criteria - in this case, the 5th record (PARKWAY Gravel). Pressing the **Find Next** button again three more times, displays the 11th, 13th and 17th record in succession.

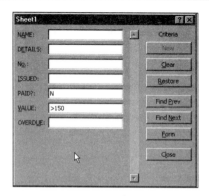

To use Excel's second method for finding and extracting data, we need to specify an area of the worksheet for setting our criteria for the search. To do this, first copy the field names of the database (A3:G3) to an empty area of the worksheet, say, A23:G23 which will form the first line of the 'criteria range'. Label this area CRITERIA FOR SEARCHING in cell A22.

Now type in cells E24 and F24 the actual criteria (N and >150), respectively, then use the **Data, Filter, Advanced Filter** command and specify in the displayed dialogue box the **List range** and **Criteria range** as A3:G20 and A23:G24 (it includes the field names in both cases). Pressing the **OK** button, causes Excel to **Filter the list in-place** by hiding the rows that do not meet the criteria, as shown below.

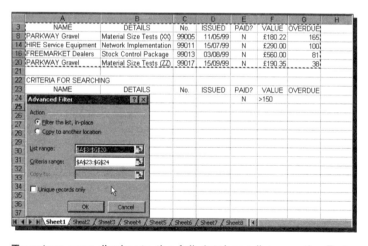

To return your display to the full database list, use the **Data, Filter, Show All** command.

Note: Do not specify an empty line as part of the criterion range, as this has the effect of searching the database for *all* records. The criteria must be entered in the second and subsequent rows of the criterion range, with each entered below the copy of the appropriate field name. A label (text) or a value may be entered exactly as it appears in the database.

In the case of searching a database for label (text), such as under the fields 'NAME' and 'DETAILS' in our example, you can use the two special characters ? and * (known as 'wildcard characters') to match any single character of a label or all characters to the end of the label, as shown below.

	A	B	C	D	E	F	G	H
3	NAME	DETAILS	No.	ISSUED	PAID?	VALUE	OVERDUE	
8	PARKWAY Gravel	Material Size Tests (XX)	99005	11/05/99	N	£180.22	165	
20	PARKWAY Gravel	Material Size Tests (ZZ)	99017	15/09/99	N	£190.35	38	
21								
22	CRITERIA FOR SEARCHING							
23	NAME	DETAILS	No.	ISSUED	PAID?	VALUE	OVERDUE	
24	Park*				N	>150		
25								

To search a database for values, either enter the value as the exact criterion or use a simple numeric comparison, such as >90, in which the logical operators (<, <=, >, >=, <>) can be used. The logical formula generates a value of 1 if the condition is TRUE or a value of 0 if the condition is FALSE.

Several criteria can be entered, either in the same row, if you want Excel to search for records that match every criterion (i.e. criteria entered are linked with the logical AND), or one per row, if you want Excel to search records that satisfy any of the criteria (i.e. criteria entered are linked with the logical OR), or a combination of the two, as shown below.

	A	B	C	D	E	F	G	H
3	NAME	DETAILS	No.	ISSUED	PAID?	VALUE	OVERDUE	
8	PARKWAY Gravel	Material Size Tests (XX)	99005	11/05/99	N	£180.22	165	
14	HIRE Service Equipment	Network Implementation	99011	15/07/99	N	£290.00	100	
16	FREEMARKET Dealers	Stock Control Package	99013	03/08/99	N	£560.00	81	
20	PARKWAY Gravel	Material Size Tests (ZZ)	99017	15/09/99	N	£190.35	38	
21								
22	CRITERIA FOR SEARCHING							
23	NAME	DETAILS	No.	ISSUED	PAID?	VALUE	OVERDUE	
24	Park*				N			
25						>150		
26								

When you finish, don't forget to use the **Data, Filter, Show All** command to display the full database list.

Extracting Records

To extract records and have them copied into another area of the worksheet, we need to select the **Copy to another location** option in the Advanced Filter dialogue box. But first, we need to set up a second area - the 'output range'. To do this, copy the field names to the cell range A28:G28 and label it as 'OUTPUT RANGE' in cell A27, as shown below.

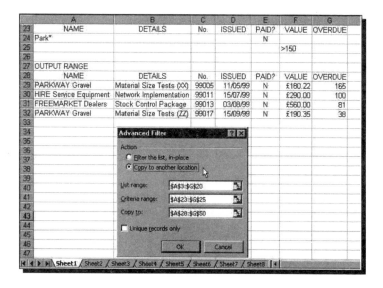

The above screen dump is a composite - it shows what action you have to take and the result of that action.

Finally, note that we chose to put the criteria and output ranges in rows below the actual database (perhaps not the best position), rather than on the side of it. This avoids the errors that might ensue should we later decide to insert a row in our database, which will also insert a row in the criteria/output range. For a more structured worksheet layout, see end of chapter.

Save this worksheet under the filename **Invoice 3**.

Structuring a Workbook

In a well designed workbook, areas of calculations using formulae should be kept on a separate sheet from the data entry sheet. The reason for this is to prevent accidental overwriting of formulae that might be contained within the data entry sheet.

As an example, we will use the **Invoice 3** file, but instead of extracting data into the same sheet, we will use another sheet into which to copy the extracted records. To do this, first open file **Invoice 3**, then use the **Window, New Window** command, followed by the **Window, Arrange** command and click the **Horizontal** radio button on the displayed dialogue box. Next, activate the lower window and click on the Sheet2 tab to display an empty worksheet at the bottom half of the screen, as shown below.

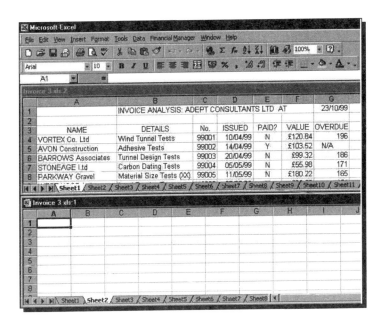

Now use the **Edit, Cut** and **Edit, Paste** commands to transfer cell range A22:G28 of Sheet1 to a range starting at cell A1 of Sheet2 and adjust the widths of the various columns to match those of Sheet1 (also, don't forget to delete from Sheet1 any extracted data from a previous search).

Note: Excel only extracts data into an active sheet. Therefore, you must make Sheet2 the active sheet, and since the program also requires to know which are the database field labels, place the cell pointer in cell A7, before you use the **Data, Filter, Advanced Filter** command. The address in the **List range** box of the Advanced Filter dialogue box must be specified (you can either type it in or use the buttons to the right of the entry box to point to the required range) to indicate the correct address for the database list which is

```
Sheet1!$A$3:$G$20
```

The **Criteria range** and the **Copy to** address locations should be similarly prefixed with Sheet2 for correct data extraction. To access the entry box of the latter, click the **Copy to another location** radio button on the Advanced Filter dialogue box, as shown below.

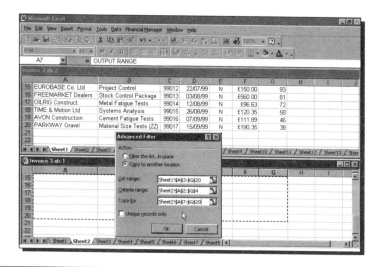

Pressing the **OK** button causes the records that match the specified criteria to be extracted from Sheet1 and copied into Sheet2, as shown below.

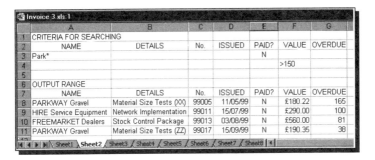

Save the resultant workbook under the filename **Invoice 4**.

Another aspect of structuring, is the provision of a screen with technical information about the contents of the particular workbook; a kind of overview of the function of the worksheet application. This area should also contain instructions for the use of the particular application at hand. Such information can help you in the future, or help others to learn and use an application easily and effectively. If you use range names, then include a range name table in your information screen(s).

Finally, provide a separate sheet within a workbook, or a separate worksheet altogether, for macros (the subject of Chapter 9), which are in a programming language that allows you to chain together menu commands. Sensitive sheets or indeed whole workbooks can be protected using the **Tools, Protection** command and either select the **Protect Sheet** or the **Protect Workbook** option, according to your application needs, to restrict cell entries to unprotected cells. This prevents accidental changes being made to cells containing formulae.

A good spreadsheet design, using the 3-dimensional ability of Excel could be as follows:

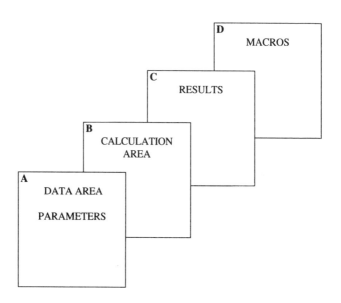

Obviously, the headings of the various workbook sheets above could be different. They would largely depend on the application at hand.

7

Other Tools and Capabilities

As well as the **Spelling** and **AutoCorrect** tools, to be found under the **Tools** menu option, Excel comes with an integrated Auditor, and tools to solve what-if type of problems such as the Goal Seek, What-if Tables, Solver and Scenarios. A short description of each of these is given below.

The Auditor

You use the Auditor to analyse the way your worksheet is structured, or for locating the source of errors in formulae.

When you invoke the Auditor by selecting the **Tools, Auditing** command, the options sub-menu is displayed, as shown below.

In this you can specify what you want to audit on the current file (for a description of the options see below), the default being **Trace Precedents**.

The Audit options have the following functions:

Option	Function
Trace precedents	Identifies all cells in the audit file that provide data for a particular formula.
Trace dependents	Identifies all formulae in the audit file that refer to a particular cell.

Trace Error	Identifies all cells involved in the production of an error, such as a circular reference.
Remove All Arrows	Removes the identifying arrows placed on the worksheet as a result of invoking the previous options.
Show Auditing Toolbar	Toggles the display of the Auditing Toolbar on and off.

As an example, we show below an audit on the file **Project 3**, for the first two options. For the first option, select cell E9, then use the **Tools, Auditing, Trace Precedents** command, while for the second option, select cell B11, then use the **Tools, Auditing, Trace Dependents** command.

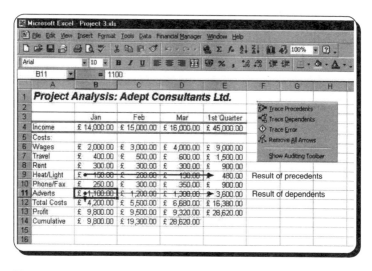

To remove the arrows resulting from the above choice of auditing options, use the **Tools, Remove All Arrows** command.

Save the file under the filename **Tools 1**, as we will be using it to illustrate the next Excel Tool.

The Goal Seek

You use the **Goal Seek** to fine-tune a formula that gives you the required result by changing one of the variables that affect the final value. As an example, we will use the information in the **Tools 1** file. If you don't have this file, use the **Project 3** file and save it as **Tools 1**.

To effectively use Goal Seek, you must adhere to the following procedure:

- Type the formula to be fine-tuned by Goal Seek in a cell. We will use the **=sum(B4:D4)** formula in cell E4 of our example.

- Invoke Goal Seek, by using the **Tools, Goal Seek** command which displays the Goal Seek dialogue box shown below.

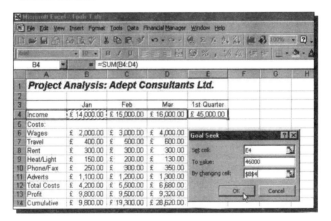

In this dialogue box you can specify in the **Set cell** box the address or range name of the cell that contains the formula you want to fine-tune, as shown above. In the **To value** box you type the value you want the formula in the formula cell to equate to when Goal Seek solves the problem, while in the **By changing cell** box you type the address of the cell whose value Goal Seek can change.

- Click the **OK** button to find an answer to the problem, displayed below (it changed the contents of B4 from £14,000 to £15,000). If it can't be done, you will be told.

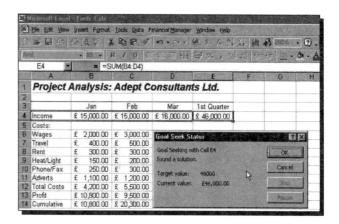

If you don't want to lose the original values in the adjustable cell, then press the **Cancel** button.

What-if Tables

What-if tables are used if you require to calculate and display the results of substituting different values for one or more (up to three) variables in a formula.

For example, suppose we wanted to examine the effect to the quarterly profits of ADEPT Consultants if we varied the quarterly income from £35,000 to £55,000, in steps of £5,000. This problem is, of course, rather trivial, but suppose at the same time we expected a wage award increase of between 0% to 3%, while all other costs were tied to inflation which could change from 3% to 5%. This becomes rather more difficult to analyse. However, using what-if tables reduces the problem to something more manageable.

A Two-Input What-if Table

To illustrate the above problem, but simplifying it by forgetting inflation, we will use the **Tools 1** file (you could use **Project 3** instead). Use the **Window, Freeze Panes** command, then fill in the range F2:K9, as shown below:

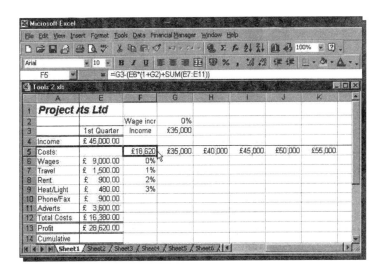

Note: A two-input what-if table has two input cells - in our example these are: Input 1 in cell G2 (which refers to the rows) and input 2 in cell G3 (which refers to the columns), representing 'Wage increases' and 'Income', respectively. The value in each of these cells is the first value in their respective ranges, which are F6:F9 and G5:K5. Thus, income varies from £35,000 to £55,000, while wage increases vary from 0% to 3%. Finally, a formula is required in cell F5 which represents profits and which refers to the two input cells defined above. The formula used is:

```
=G3-(E6*(1+G2)+SUM(E7:E11))
```

To verify that this formula is correct, change the input in the 'Income' cell (G3) to £45,000, which should give you the same profit in cell F5 as that shown in cell E13.

The formula in a two-input what-if table must be placed in the top-left corner of the table. Which cell is declared as a 'row input' and a 'column input' in the Table dialogue box is very important.

In the case of a one-input what-if table, Excel expects the input range to be either in one column, with the formula placed at the top of the next column to the right of the input column, or in one row, with the formula placed at the top of the next row to the left of the input row.

Before proceeding with the analysis of our problem, save your work under the filename **Tools 2**, then select the effective table range F5:K9 by highlighting it. Next, use the **Data, Table** command and enter G3 in the **Row Input cell** box of the displayed dialogue box, and G2 in the **Column Input Cell** box, as shown below:

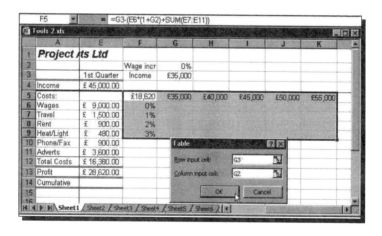

Pressing the **OK** button, displays the results shown on the next page. You could now save this example under the filename **Tools 3**.

	A	E	F	G	H	I	J	K
1	*Project its Ltd*							
2			Wage incr	0%				
3		1st Quarter	Income	£35,000				
4	Income	£ 45,000.00						
5	Costs:		£18,620	£35,000	£40,000	£45,000	£50,000	£55,000
6	Wages	£ 9,000.00	0%	18620	23620	28620	33620	38620
7	Travel	£ 1,500.00	1%	18530	23530	28530	33530	38530
8	Rent	£ 900.00	2%	18440	23440	28440	33440	38440
9	Heat/Light	£ 480.00	3%	18350	23350	28350	33350	38350
10	Phone/Fax	£ 900.00						
11	Adverts	£ 3,600.00						
12	Total Costs	£ 16,380.00						
13	Profit	£ 28,620.00						
14	Cumulative							

Sheet1 / Sheet2 / Sheet3 / Sheet4 / Sheet5 / Sheet6

Editing a Data Table

The input values and formula in the top leftmost column of a data table can be edited at any time. However, the actual results calculated within the data table cannot be edited individually, because they are an array. Some editing operations require you to select the entire data table, while others require you to select only the resulting values. For example:

- To clear the resulting values from a data table, select the resulting values only (G6:G9 in our example) and press the <Del> key. Individual resulting values cannot be cleared separately.

- To copy resulting values from a data table, select them and use the **Edit, Copy** command. Doing this results in copying the values only, not the formulae for those values. Subsequent use of the **Paste Special** command converts the resulting values array into a range of constant values.

- To move, delete, or modify a table, first select the entire data table (F5:K9 in our example). If you are moving the table, having selected it, then click the border of the selection and drag it to a new location on your worksheet.

The Solver

You use the Solver if you want to analyse data in a worksheet and solve 'what-if' type of problems. Solver is ideal for problems that have more than one answer. It can investigate different options and present you with alternative solutions, including the best match to your requirements.

Before you can use the Solver, you might need to install it, as it is an add-in and it might not have been installed automatically by SETUP - you will know if it is installed already as its name will then appear amongst the options of the **Tools** drop-down menu. If it does not, you will need to install it using the **Tools, Add-Ins** command which opens the dialogue box shown to the left. Next, scroll down to the **Solver Add-in** option, check it and press the **OK** button. The program will tell you that this add-in is not installed and you will be asked whether you would like to install it now. To do so, you must have the Office 2000 distribution CDs to hand, and follow the instructions on the screen.

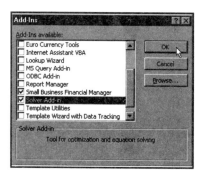

To use the Solver option, you start with a worksheet model. Solver problems can be set up in one or more worksheet files in memory, by selecting which cells to adjust, adding logical formulae, and defining the limits of the required answers.

As an example, let us analyse more closely Adept Consultants' 1st Quarter results. We use the information held in Sheet1 of the **Tools 1** file (you could use the **Project 3** file instead). On a Sheet other than Sheet1 of either file, add the information shown on the next page and save the resultant workbook under the filename **Tools 4**.

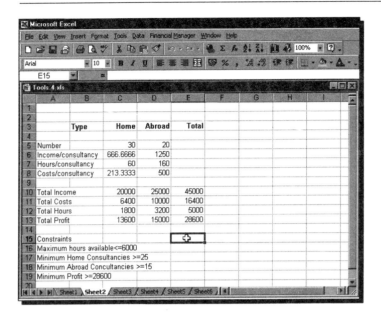

What we assume here is that Adept Consultants operate both at home and abroad. In the first quarter they undertook 30 consultancies at home and 20 consultancies abroad. The range C5:D8 holds numerical information on the income, hours taken, and the costs per consultancy, respectively.

In range C10:D13 we have entered formulae to calculate the total income, costs, hours spent, and profit made from each type of consultancy from information held in range C5:D8, while range E10:E13 summates the two types of consultancies.

Cells E12 and E13 hold the total time spent in consultancies and the total profit made, respectively, which is very important information.

What we would like to do now is to increase the consultancies to make up the maximum available time in the three month period, which is 6000 hours, while maximising the profit. The question is 'what mixture of consultancies (home or abroad) is more profitable?'

Starting the Solver

To start Solver use the **Tools, Solver** command, which displays the following Solver Parameters dialogue box:

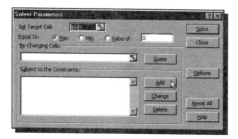

Next, we would like to enter the constraints under which we will impose a solution to our problem. These can be added, changed or deleted using the three buttons at the bottom of the Solver Parameters dialogue box shown above.

Entering Constraints

At the bottom of the worksheet, we have included certain constraints, discussed below, which are entered as logical formulae in the range E16:E19 using the Add Constraint dialogue box, shown here, by clicking the **Add** button on the

Solver Parameters dialogue box. After entering each one of these, press the **Add** button so that you can enter the next one.

The logic behind these constraints is as follows:

- Since the maximum available hours in a quarter must remain less than or equal to 6000 hours, we enter in cell E16 the formula **E12<=6000**.

- Since a long term contract with the government requires that at least 25 consultancies are undertaken at home, we enter in cell E17 the formula **C5>=25**.

- Since a similar long term contract with a foreign government requires that at least 15 consultancies are undertaken abroad, we enter in cell E18 the formula **D5>=15**.

- Since we would like to maximise profits, we enter in cell E19 the formula **E13>=28600**.

Solving a Problem

Once the last constraint is inserted into the Add Constraint dialogue box, pressing the **OK** button opens the Solver Preferences box, shown below.

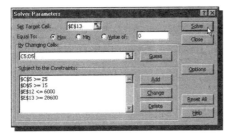

Next, specify the **Set Target Cell**, as E13, then the adjustable cells in the **By Changing Cells** box as C5:D5 - these are cells that contain values that Solver can adjust when it searches for an answer.

Finally, press the **Solve** button and let Solver find a solution, place the answer in the worksheet and display the Solver Results dialogue box, as shown below.

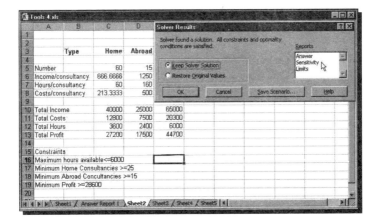

You now have a choice of either keeping the values found by Solver, or reverting to the original worksheet values. Also from the **Reports** section of the dialogue box you can choose to display one of three report types: Answer, Sensitivity, and Limits. Selecting one of these causes Excel to produce an appropriate report and place it in a separate Sheet. Below, we show the results for an Answer Report.

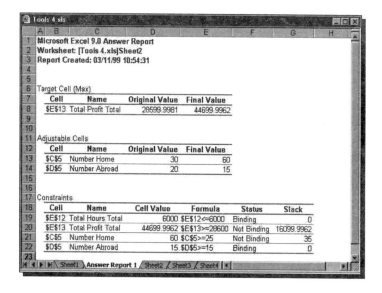

Finally, save your work under the filename **Tools 5**.

If a problem is too complex for the default settings of Solver, then click the **Options** button on the Solver Parameters dialogue box to display the Solver Options dialogue box, in which you can change the time limit for solving a problem, the maximum iterations allowed, and even select the type of model to be used.

Managing What-if Scenarios

There are times when we would like to examine different what-if scenarios created from a single spreadsheet model. Normally, managers tend to copy the model to different parts of the spreadsheet so as to examine and display different assumptions. However, keeping track of all the different assumptions can become extremely problematic, mostly confusing, and indeed wasteful of spreadsheet space and, therefore, computer memory.

With Excel you can use the Scenario Manager to keep all the different versions of the same worksheet model together. In addition, you can also give each version a meaningful name, such as 'Original Case', 'Best Case', and 'Worst Case'.

To illustrate the method, we will use the **Tools 5** example which we employed when discussing the Solver. In addition, we assume that it is possible to reduce the number of hours it takes Adept Consultants to complete a consultancy at home or abroad, but if one is reduced the other is increased by the same amount.

The model looks as shown on the next page, with '% Changes' added in columns F and G, the contents of cells C7 and D7 changed to =60*(1+F7) and =160*(1+G7), respectively, and the overall profit now also displayed in column H, by inserting in H5 the reference =E13. Obviously, since we will be optimising our solutions, you must learn to use Solver first.

Next, enter 0% change on the hours per consultancy on both the home and abroad input cells, which reflects the 'Original' state of our problem with an optimum answer on profits using the already defined constraints. This gives a profit of £44,700 - the no change scenario.

Finally, save your model as **Tools 6** before going on. This ensures that you can go back to it if anything goes wrong when trying to run the **Scenarios** option.

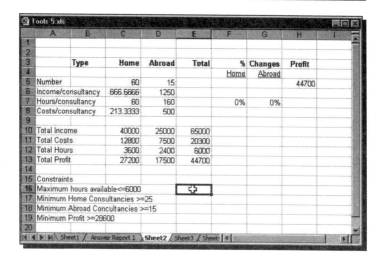

Next, use the **Tools, Scenarios** command to display the Scenario Manager dialogue box which, at this point, contains no scenarios. To start the process, press the **Add** button to display the Add Scenario dialogue box shown below.

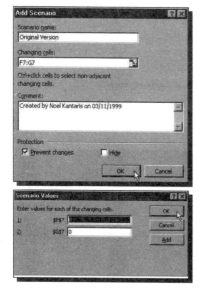

Now add the description 'Original Version' in the **Scenario name** text box, then specify in the **Changing cells** F7:G7 and press the **OK** button to display the Scenario Values dialogue box, shown below, with the values for both F7 and G7 showing as 0 (zero). Pressing the **OK** button returns you to the Scenario Manager dialogue box with the recently created scenario appearing in the **Scenarios** list box.

Next, repeat the process by pressing the **Add** button on the Scenario Manager dialogue box to display the Add Scenario dialogue box in which you type a name for the second scenario, say 'Negative Home Change'. Then, change the values for cells F7 and G7 to –5% and 5%, respectively, in the Scenario Values dialogue box (the actual values should be entered as -0.05 and 0.05).

Finally, repeat the process to create a 'Positive Home Change' with Scenario Values in F7 and G7 of 5% and –5%, respectively.

To see and select any one of the defined scenarios, use the Scenario Manager dialogue box, shown below (activated by the **Tools, Scenarios** command), with all the different versions of the solutions listed. To look at the results of one of these, simply highlight it and press the **Show** button.

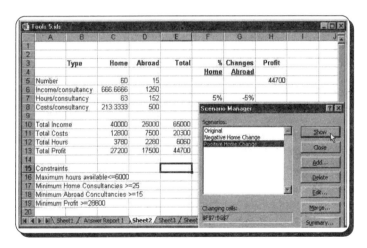

Last but not least, Scenario Manager allows you to merge several versions together and define them as a scenario, and also create a summary report - you have a choice of two. The first report is a 'scenario summary', while the second is a 'scenario pivot table'. With the pivot table you get an instant what-if analysis of different scenario combinations.

Finally, save your work under the filename **Tools 7**.

8

Sharing Information

You can link or embed all or part of an existing file created either in an Office application or in any other application that supports Object Linking and Embedding (OLE). However, if an application does not support OLE, then you must use the copy/cut and paste commands to copy or move information from one application to another. In general, you copy, move, link, embed, or hyperlink information depending on the imposed situation, as follows:

Imposed Situation	Method to Adopt
Inserted information will not need updating, or Application does not support OLE.	Copy or move
Inserted information needs to be automatically updated in the destination file as changes are made to the data in the source file, or Source file will always be available and you want to minimise the size of the destination file, or Source file is to be shared amongst several users.	Link
Inserted information might need to be updated but source file might not be always accessible, or Destination files needs to be edited without having these changes reflected in the source file.	Embed
To jump to a location in a document or Web page, or to a file that was created in a different program.	Hyperlink

Copying or Moving Information

To copy or move information between programs running under Windows, such as Microsoft applications, is extremely easy. To move information, use the drag and drop facility, while to copy information, use the **Edit, Copy** and **Edit, Paste** commands.

To illustrate the technique, we will use a file created in Lotus 1-2-3 containing the solution of a 'Compound Interest' problem. We will consider the following two possibilities:

Source File Available without Application

We assume that you only have the source file **Comp_Int.WK4** on disc, but not the application that created it (that is you don't have Lotus 1-2-3). In such a situation, you can only copy the contents of the whole file to the destination (in our case an Excel worksheet). To achieve this, do the following:

- Start Excel and minimise it on the Taskbar.

- Use My Computer (or Windows Explorer) to locate the file whose contents you want to copy into an Excel workbook.

- Click the filename that you want to copy, hold the mouse button down and point to Excel on the Taskbar until the application opens.

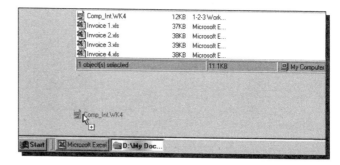

- While still holding the mouse button down, move the mouse pointer into Excel's open worksheet to the point where you would like to insert the contents of **Comp_Int.WK4**.

- Release the mouse button to place the contents of **Comp_Int.WK4** into Excel at that point.

The result is shown below. As you can see, Excel has preserved the formatting styles contained in the Lotus 1-2-3 file, and also drawn a chart automatically, placing it on a separate sheet which we renamed 'Graph'.

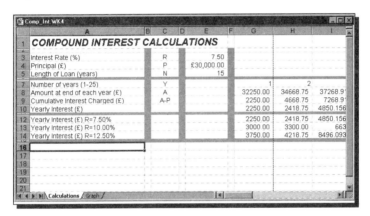

Clicking the **Graph** sheet, reveals the following:

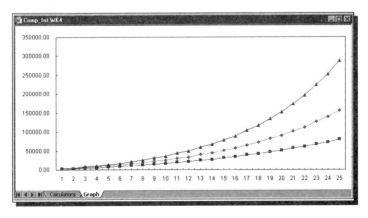

Source File and Application Available

Assuming that you have both the file and the application that created it on your computer, you can copy all or part of the contents of the source file to the destination file. Here we also consider two possibilities:

To copy part of a spreadsheet file (in our case part of **Comp_Int.WK4**) into an Excel workbook, do the following:

- Start your source spreadsheet (whichever you happened to use - in our case it is Lotus 1-2-3 Release 9) and open your worksheet.

- Highlight as much information as you would like to copy into Excel, and click the copy icon on the Toolbar (or use the **Edit, Copy** command).

- Start Excel and place the cell indicator where you would like the data to appear and click the Paste icon on the Toolbar (or use the **Edit, Paste** command).

The result is shown below. Note that all the columns have the same width - you will have to change these appropriately, and the formulae in your original worksheet did not copy across - only the displayed values.

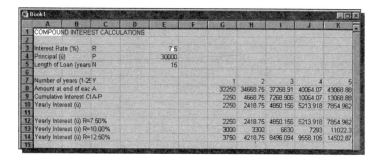

However, normally we tend to want to incorporate part of an Excel worksheet into a word processed document. This document might have been created in Word 2000, or any other Windows word processor.

To copy part of an Excel worksheet (say **Project 3**) into a document, do the following:

- Start Excel and open **Project 3**.

- Highlight as much information as you would like to copy and click the copy icon on the Toolbar (or use the **Edit**, **Copy** command).

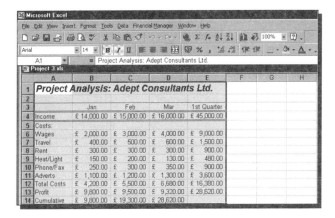

- Start your word processor, place the insertion pointer at the desired place, and click the Paste icon on the Toolbar (or use the **Edit**, **Paste** command).

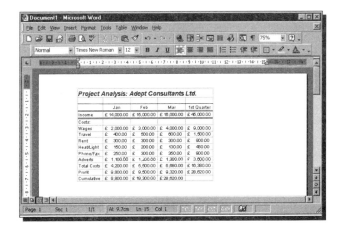

Inserting an Excel Worksheet in Word

If the 'Insert Excel Worksheet' button, shown here, appears

on your Word 2000 Toolbar, you can use it to insert a worksheet of the required number of rows and columns, by simply clicking the button and dragging down to the right. As you drag the mouse, the 'Worksheet' button expands to create the grid of rows and columns, shown below, in a similar manner to that of creating rows and columns of tables.

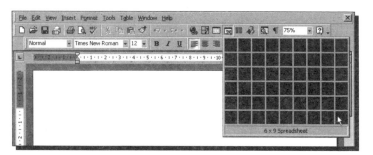

When you release the mouse button, the worksheet is inserted in your Word document. You can then insert data and apply functions to them. To see which functions are available, click the Paste Function button.

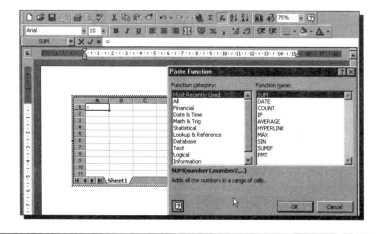

Object Linking and Embedding

Object Linking is copying information from one file (the source file) to another file (the destination file) and maintaining a connection between the two files. When information in the source file is changed, then the information in the destination file is automatically updated. Linked data is stored in the source file, while the file into which you place the data stores only the location of the source and displays a representation of the linked data.

For example, you would use Object Linking if you would want an Excel chart included in, say, a Word document to be updated whenever you changed the information used to create the chart in the first place within Excel. In such a case, the Excel worksheet containing the chart would be referred to as the source file, while the Word document would be referred to as the destination file.

Object Embedding is inserting information created in one file (the source file) into another file (the container file). After such information has been embedded, the object becomes part of the container file. When you double-click an embedded object, it opens in the application in which it was created in the first place. You can then edit it in place, and the original object in the source application remains unchanged.

Thus, the main differences between linking and embedding are where the data is stored and how it is updated after you place it in your file. Linking saves you disc space as only one copy of the linked object is kept on disc. Embedding a logo chosen for your headed paper, saves the logo with every saved letter!

In what follows, we will discuss how you can link or embed either an entire file or selected information from an existing file, and how you can edit an embedded object.

Embedding a New Object

To embed a new object into an application, do the following:

- Open the container file, say **Project 3**, and click where you want to embed the new object.

- Use the **Insert, Picture** command, to display the

additional drop-down menu, shown here. From this last drop-down menu action **Clip Art**, click the category you want and select a graphic. As an example, we selected **Clip Art** (you could select a different option) and chose the Buttons & Icons category from which we selected the graphic shown below. Clicking the **Insert Clip** button on the drop-down menu, embeds the selected object within Excel.

- Size the inserted picture and place it where you want it to appear in your worksheet.

If you were able to follow our suggestions, your worksheet should now look as shown below. Do try it for yourself.

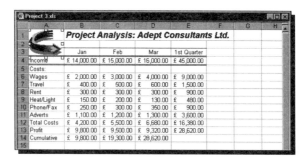

Should you want to change a picture you have inserted into your document, use the **Picture** toolbar that opens when you inserted the picture. The tools on this bar can be used to manipulate pictures to suit your needs. Their functions are as follows:

Insert Picture from File

Image Control

More Contrast

Less Contrast

More Brightness

Less Brightness

Crop

Line Style

Format Picture

Set Transparent Colour

Reset Picture

Try using these tools on the imported image to see how you can enhance or utterly destroy it! If, at the end of the day, you don't save it, it doesn't matter what you do to it. Just experiment.

If all is well, save this worksheet under the filename **Share 1**.

Linking or Embedding an Existing File

To embed an existing, say Word 2000, file in its entirety into
Excel 2000, do the following:

- Open the container file, say **Project 3**, and click
  where you want to embed the Word file.

- Use the **Insert, Object** command, to open the Object
  dialogue box, shown below, when the **Create from
  File** tab is clicked.

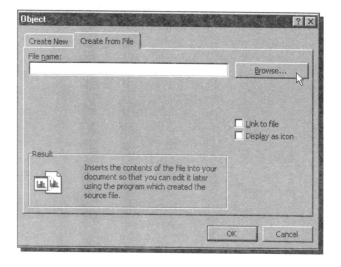

To locate the file you want to link or embed, click **Browse**,
and then select the options you want.

- In the **File name** box, type the name of the file you
  want to link or embed (we used one typed into Word
  and named **Testdoc.doc**).

- If you wanted to maintain a link to the original file,
  check the **Link to file** box.

Finally, click the **OK** button to embed your Word file into
Excel. The result is shown on the next page.

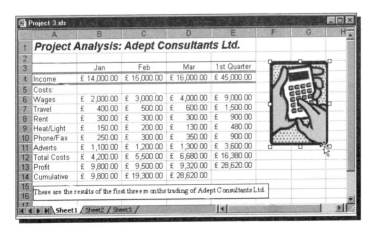

Note: To insert graphics files into an Excel worksheet, use the **Insert, Picture, From File** command instead of the **Insert, Object** command. This opens up the Insert Picture dialogue box which allows you to specify within a **Look in** box the folder and file you want to insert.

As an example, we used below the **Insert, Picture, From File** command while **Project 3** was opened, and selected the **Account.bmp** file from Microsoft's Clipart folder.

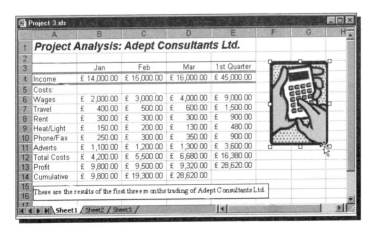

Save this Excel worksheet under the filename **Share 2**.

Editing an Embedded Object

If the application in which you created an embedded object is installed on your computer, double-click the object to open it for editing. Some applications start the original application in a separate window and then open the object for editing, while other applications temporarily replace the menus and toolbars in the current application so that you can edit the embedded object in place, without switching to another window.

If the application in which you created an embedded object is not installed on your computer, convert the object to the file format of an application you do have. For example, if your word processed document contains an embedded Microsoft Works Spreadsheet object and you do not have Works, you can convert the object to an Excel Workbook format and edit it in Excel.

Some embedded objects, such as sound and video clips, when double-clicked start playing their contents, instead of opening an application for editing. To illustrate this, use the **Insert, Object** command to open the Object dialogue box shown below with the Create from File tab pressed.

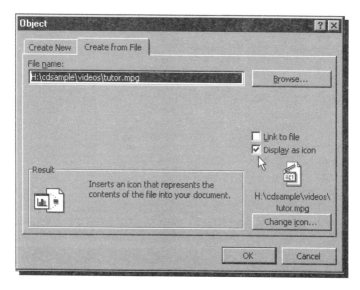

Next, check the **Displ̲ay as icon** box, browse to the location of the required file, and insert it into your document. In the example below we used both the **tutor.mpg** media file from its folder in the Windows 98 CD and the **goodtime.mpg** video file from its folder in the Windows 95 CD, then saved the resultant workbook under the filename **Share 3**. The **tutor** file is to be found in the **cdsample, videos, mpeg** folder, while the **goodtime** file is to be found in the **funstuff, videos, highperf** folder. Inserting either of these places a Windows Media Player icon in your document, as shown below. Double-clicking such an icon, starts the video.

To edit one of these objects, select it and either right-click it to open the quick menu shown here, or use the **Edit {Media**

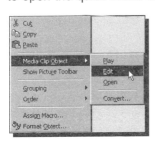

Clip Object}, Edit command. What appears within the curly brackets in this command, depends on the selected object; media clip in this case. If your embedded object was a sound clip, instead of a video, then the **Edit** menu would change to **Wave Sound O̲bject**.

Of course, unless you have the facilities required for editing such objects, you will be unable to do so.

Hyperlinks

Excel 2000 workbooks and other Office 2000 documents can be made more interesting by inserting hyperlinks to other items. A hyperlink causes a jump to another location in the current document or Web page, to a different document or Web page, or to a file that was created in a different program. You can, for example, jump from an Excel workbook to a Word document or to a PowerPoint slide to see more detail.

A hyperlink is represented by a 'hot' image or by display text (which is often blue and underlined) that you click to jump to a different location. To insert a hyperlink into a Workbook, a document, or a Web page, select the display text or image, and either use the **Insert, Hyperlink** command

or click the Insert Hyperlink icon on the Standard Toolbar, shown here. Either action opens a dialogue box which allows you to browse for the destination address.

To illustrate the procedure, start Excel, open the **Project 4** file, and type in cell B17 the words 'Yearly costs', as shown below.

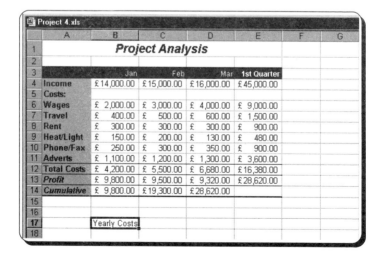

While cell B17 is the active cell, click the Hyperlink icon on the Toolbar and locate the **Project 9** file using the **File** button under the **Browse for** entry in the displayed Insert Hyperlink dialogue box shown below. Once you have located the file, its filename is inserted in the **Type the file or Web page name** box, and pressing the **OK** button inserts a hyperlink to that location.

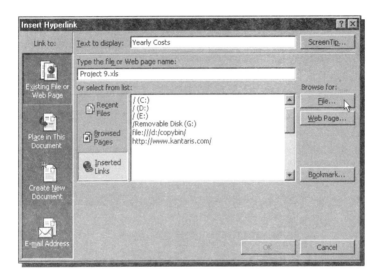

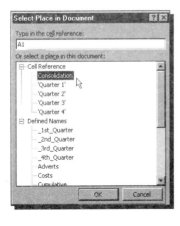

Should you want to jump to a specific sheet or defined name within a workbook, click the **Bookmark** button which opens the Select Place in Document dialogue box shown to the left. In the latter case, when you jump to the specified document, the cell range of the selected defined name will be highlighted automatically, a rather useful feature.

Pressing the **OK** button of each dialogue box, underlines the text in B17, as shown below, and changes its colour to blue.

Pointing to such a hyperlink, changes the mouse pointer to a hand, as shown here to the left, and left-clicking it, displays the 'Consolidation' Sheet of the **Project 9** file. When you have finished looking at this file, click the Back icon on the Web Toolbar, shown below, for the program to return you automatically to the hyperlinked Excel workbook.

If the location of the file you wanted to hyperlink to is incorrect, then errors will obviously occur. Save your work under the filename **Share 4**.

To remove unwanted hyperlinks, right-click the hyperlinked cell, select the **Hyperlink** option of the drop-down menu, then choose the **Remove Hyperlink** sub-menu option.

As you can see from the above discussion, hyperlinks can just as easily be created and used on Web pages, provided you have Internet access either through your intranet or through a modem and an account with an Internet Service Provider (ISP for short). The procedure is identical to creating a hyperlink between two files on your hard disc.

Hypertext links on a Web page are elements that you can click with the left mouse button to jump to another Web document. You are actually fetching another file to your PC, and the link is an address that uniquely identifies the location of the target file, wherever it may be. This address is known as a Uniform Resource Locator (URL for short).

How to use Excel on the Internet is the subject of the next chapter.

9

Excel and the Internet

Microsoft has tried to integrate Excel 2000 with the Internet
and the Web, by allowing the creation of the following:

- Non-interactive data or charts.

- Interactive spreadsheets, PivotTable lists, or charts.

- Combination Web pages.

The first one of these lets users view data as they would in
Microsoft Excel, including tabs for each worksheet that they
can click to switch between worksheets. It is like publishing a
'snapshot' of the data, but users can not interact with the
data.

To view non-interactive data or charts on the Web, users
only need a Web browser - no restrictions on the type of
browser. Also, they don't need Excel 2000 on their computer.

The last two items on the list above allow the user to
interact with all or some of the data on your Web page. Such
a Web page is created from a Microsoft Excel worksheet, or
items from it, by saving the data with 'spreadsheet
functionality'. Publishing in this way, allows users to enter,
format, calculate, analyse, sort and filter data.

Interactive Web pages allow users to change the data and
layout of Web page items. It is used if you have data that
users want to recalculate. For example, if you are supplying a
program to calculate the repayments on loans based on
particular interest rates (see example on page 148).

To view interactive (or partially interactive) data on the
Web, users need to have installed on their computer the
Microsoft Office 2000 Web Components, and must also be
using the Microsoft Internet Explorer version 4.01 or later.

Creating Excel Static Web Pages

Most Web pages are written in HTML (Hypertext Markup Language), which can be used by Web browsers on any operating system, such as Windows, Macintosh, and UNIX.

Entire Workbook on a Web Page

Excel allows you to put an entire workbook on a Web page. As an example, we will use the **Project 9.xls** file which has several worksheets, including three charts saved in their individual sheets. To do this, start Excel, then

- Open **Project 9**, and use the **File, Save as Web Page** command to display the dialogue box below.

- In the **Save in** box, locate the drive, folder, Web folder, Web server, or FTP location where you want to save your Web page (we chose our WorkBooks folder).

- Make sure that the **Entire Workbook** radio button is selected, then click the **Change Title** button to display the Set Page Title dialogue box. Type a description which will be displayed in the titlebar of the browser.

- Finally, press the **Save** button. To see the result of your efforts, use your Web browser, and locate the **.htm** file produced by the save command. In our case this file was called **Project 9.htm** by default. Opening this file displays the following:

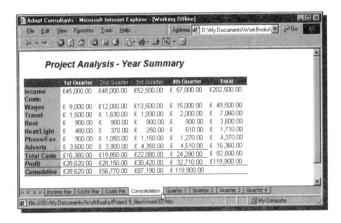

Note the workbook tabs at the bottom of your browser. These are similar to the tabs of an Excel workbook, except that when you point at them with the mouse pointer their full path is displayed in the Status bar below. From this you will see that all the original Excel sheets are held in a **_file** folder, called the 'supporting files folder' (in our case **Project 9_file**). Also note that charts are saved in Graphics Interchange Format (**.gif**) image files in the supporting files folder.

Most of the features and formatting in your workbook are retained if you open your Web page (**.htm**) file in Microsoft Excel later. However, certain formatting, such as defined custom views, references to consolidation data, labels in formulae that were converted to cell references, scenarios you created, shared workbook information, or any defined function categories, are not retained. So if you want to change data in your Web site created as non-interactive, then update the original **.xls** file in Excel and republish.

Single Worksheet on a Web Page

Excel allows you to put a single worksheet on a Web page. As an example, we will use again the **Project 9.xls** file, but this time we will only save the Consolidation worksheet on our Web page. To do this, start Excel, then

- Open **Project 9**, and use the **File, Save as Web Page** command to display the dialogue box below.

- In the **Save in** box, locate the drive, folder, Web folder, Web server, or FTP location where you want to save your Web page (we chose our WorkBooks folder).

- Make sure that the **Selection: Sheet** radio button is chosen which causes the default **Page.htm** filename to appear in the **File name** box. Next, click the **Change Title** button to display the Set Page Title dialogue box and type a description which will be displayed in the titlebar of the browser.

- Next, press the **Publish** button which causes Excel to display the Publish as Web Page dialogue box, shown on the next page. Finally, select the item you want from the **Choose** list (in our example we selected 'Items on Consolidation'), and press the **Publish** button.

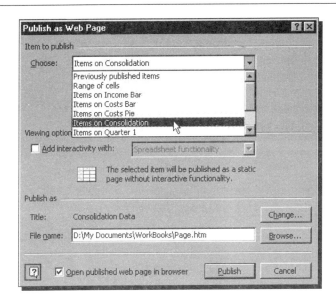

- Excel formats your chosen worksheet into a Web page and displays it in your browser, if the **Open published web page in browser** option is checked, as follows:

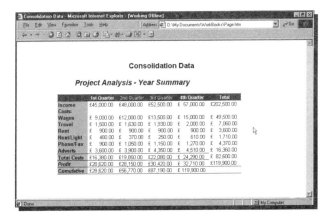

Note that the same restrictions on formatting apply, if you later change the **.htm** file in Excel (see bottom of page 145).

Creating Excel Interactive Web Pages

To illustrate this procedure, first construct an Excel example suitable for interactive Web page publishing. We chose below to create a loans repayment worksheet using the compound interest formula given as

$$A = P * (1+R/100)^Y$$

where P is the principal (original money) lent, and A is what it amounts to in time Y years at an interest rate R% per annum.

We carry out the calculation on a yearly basis to the full period of the loan (N=15 years) which can not be varied, with a value of Principal (P=£30,000) and with an interest rate (R=5%) both of which can be varied by the user in cells C4 and C3, respectively. Cells A9:A23 hold the period of the loan (1-15), while cells C9:C23 hold the result of the calculation. Hint - type in C9 the Excel formula =$C$4*(1+$C$3/100)^A9, then copy it into the range C10:C23.

Finally, we also created on the same worksheet a line chart of the repayment amount at the end of each year for the specified interest rate. The resultant Excel worksheet, saved as **Loan Repayment.xls**, is shown below.

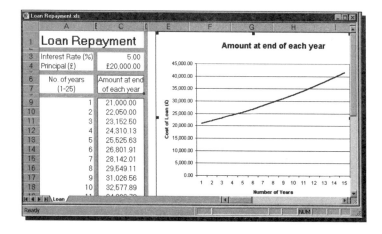

Next, use the **File, Save as Web Page** command to display the Save As dialogue box shown below.

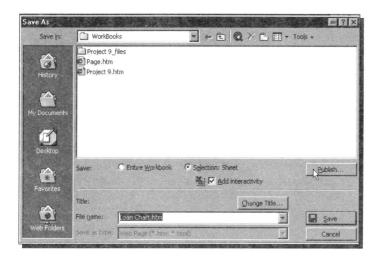

Then follow the procedure discussed previously, namely,

- In the **Save in** box, locate the drive, folder, Web folder, Web server, or FTP location where you want to save your Web page (we chose our WorkBooks folder).

- Make sure that both the **Selection: Sheet** radio button and the **Add interactivity** box are selected, then change the default **Page.htm** filename which appears in the **File name** box to **Loan Chart.htm**, and press the **Publish** button.

- Finally, in the displayed Publish as Web Page dialogue box, select **Chart** from the **Choose** list, check the **Add interactivity with** box which cause the words 'Chart functionality' to appear in the adjacent text box, check the **Open published web page in browser** box, and press the **Publish** button.

When a chart is published interactively, Excel automatically includes the source data for the chart on the Web page and includes an interactive spreadsheet control, as shown below.

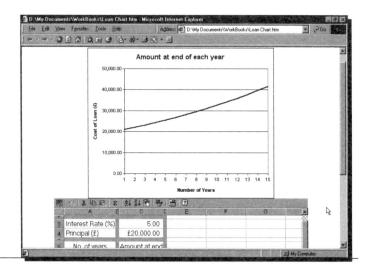

Users can not change the chart directly, but when they change the data in the spreadsheet on the Web page, the corresponding chart is updated automatically.

To change the size of the chart on the Web page, open the Web page in Microsoft FrontPage 2000 and make the changes there.

Saving Excel Web pages interactively might lose some features and formatting. These are too many to list here, but you can find them easily with the Help system. To do this, use the **Help, Microsoft Excel Help** command, and in the displayed dialogue box, shown below, search the Answer Wizard for 'Limitations on interactive Web pages'. There are several pages on this subject which are worth looking at.

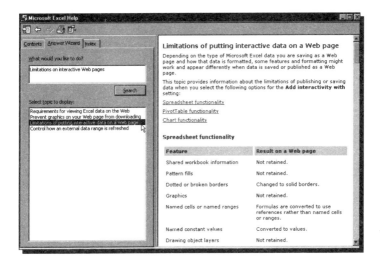

There is one topic that we found missing from the list of the chart functionality section which is that 'x-y scatter' charts do not show either the points or the lines joining those points on the chart when published on a Web page. This omission cost us some wasted time, so beware!

Retrieving Data from a Web Page

You can get data from an intranet or an FTP site on the Web by using a Web query. Excel 2000 comes with a number of built-in Web queries which you can use, or you can create your own. Of course, to get data from a Web site, you must have Internet access either through your intranet or through a modem and an account with an Internet Service Provider (ISP).

To use one of the built-in Web queries, use the **Data**, **Get**

External Data command, and select **Run Saved Query** as shown here, which opens the Saved Query dialogue box shown below.

Next, select the Web query you want to run (we chose the 'Microsoft Investor Currency Rates') and press the **Get Data** button.

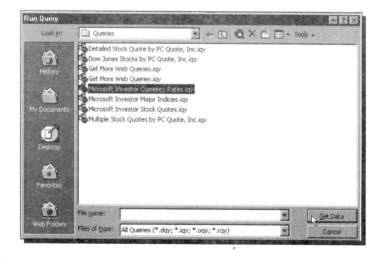

Note that a Web query has an **.iqy** filename extension. When the Returning External Data to Microsoft Excel dialogue box appears, you can select to either return the data from the Web page to the **Existing worksheet** by clicking the cell where you want to place the upper-left corner of the external data range, or return the data to a **New worksheet**.

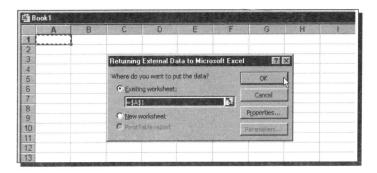

When you press the **OK** button, Excel runs the query. A spinning refresh icon appears in the Status bar to indicate that the query is running. In our case, the following data was retrieved

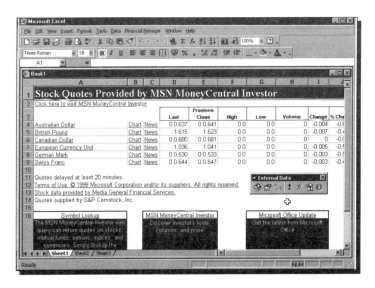

Interactive PivotTable Lists

Publishing interactive PivotTable lists on the Web is similar to publishing an interactive worksheet. A PivotTable list is an interactive table that you can use to quickly summarise large amounts of data. You use PivotTable reports when you want to compare related totals or when you want Microsoft Excel to do the sorting, subtotalling, and totalling for you.

Publishing interactively with PivotTable functionality, allows users to filter the data in the resulting PivotTable list, analyse the data by getting different views of it, and refreshing external data in a browser.

There is a wealth of information in the Microsoft Help system relating to the publishing and usage of PivotTable lists. If you need to find out more, search Help for 'PivotTable' and go through the various listed topics. Below, we show one screen dealing with this information.

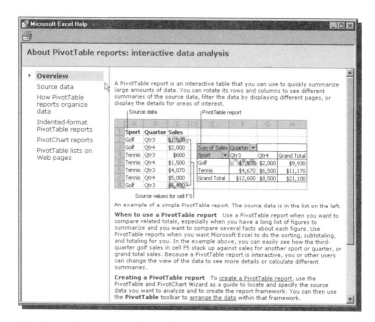

We leave it to you to investigate this subject. Have fun!

10

Customising Excel 2000

Customising Toolbars and Menus

What follows is a detailed account of how you can customise both toolbars and menus to your specific requirements, including the creation of your own toolbar.

Excel 2000, as well as all the other components of Office 2000, provide you with 'intelligent' toolbars and menus that monitor the way you work and make sure that the tools you use most often are available to you. However, if you want to use some new tool which is not on a displayed toolbar or menu, you are in trouble - you will have to look for it amongst a wealth of tools which can be activated in a number of different ways! What we will try to do here, is to show you how you could increase your working efficiency, in the shortest possible time.

The Default Toolbars and Menus

A toolbar can contain buttons with images, menus, or a combination of both. Excel includes many built-in toolbars that you can show and hide as needed by using the **View, Toolbars** command which opens the cascade menu shown to the left. To activate a toolbar, left-click it, which causes a small check mark to appear against it. By default, the Standard and Formatting built-in toolbars are docked side by side below the menu bar.

You can move toolbars by dragging the move handle on a docked toolbar, shown to the right, or drag the title bar on a floating toolbar to another location. If you drag the toolbar to the edge of the program window or to a location beside another docked toolbar, it becomes a docked toolbar.

As we have seen in earlier chapters, when you first start Excel, both active toolbars and short menus display standard buttons and basic commands. As you work with the program, the buttons and commands that you use most often are displayed on the toolbars and short menus. Both toolbars and menus can be expanded to show more buttons and commands by simply clicking the ░ (**More Buttons**) at the end of the toolbar, or the ▾ (double-arrow) at the bottom of the short menu.

To show the full set of buttons on a toolbar, drag the toolbar to a location other than the edge of the program window. To see more toolbars than those displayed when using the **View, Toolbars** command, use the **Tools, Customize** command to open the Customize dialogue box shown below, but with the Toolbars tab clicked.

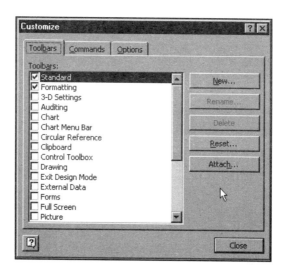

To show the full set of menu commands, click the Options tab of the Customize dialogue box, shown above, then check and/or uncheck options as required.

Move or Copy Toolbar Buttons

If you wish to move or copy a toolbar button from one toolbar to another, use the **View**, **Toolbars** command and check both toolbars, so they are visible on your screen. Then do one of the following:

*   To move a toolbar button, hold down the <Alt> key and drag the button to the new location on the same toolbar or onto another toolbar.

*   To copy a toolbar button, hold down both the <Ctrl+Alt> keys and drag the button to the new location.

Add or Remove Toolbar Buttons

To add a button to a toolbar, first display the toolbar in question, then use the **Tools**, **Customize** command to open the Customize dialogue box, shown below, with the Commands tab selected.

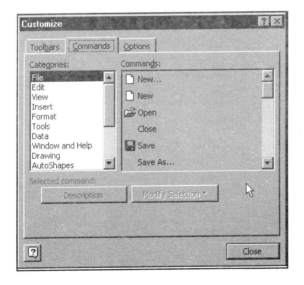

Then do the following:

- In the **Categories** box, click a category for the command you want the button to perform. For example, click Edit to add a button that performs an edit command, click Drawing to add a button to perform a drawing command, click Forms to add a button that helps with form design, or click Macros to add a button that runs a macro.

- Drag the command or macro you want from the **Commands** box to the displayed toolbar.

Note: The last choice in the **Categories** box, allows you to build your own New Menu option.

To quickly add a built-in button to a built-in toolbar, click on ▮ (**More Buttons**) on a docked toolbar (or click the ▭ (down-arrow) in the upper-left corner of a floating toolbar, then click **Add or Remove Buttons** and select the check box next to the button you want to add.

To remove a button from a displayed toolbar, hold the <Alt> button down and drag the unwanted button from its position on the toolbar on to the editing area of your document. When you remove a built-in toolbar button, the button is still available in the Customize dialogue box. However, when you remove a custom toolbar button, it is permanently deleted. To remove and save a custom toolbar button for later use, you should create a 'storage toolbar' as described below.

Create a Custom Toolbar

To create a custom toolbar, carry out the following steps:

- Display the toolbars that contain the buttons (whether custom or built-in buttons) you want to copy, move, or store in a custom toolbar.

- Use the **Tools**, **Customize** command, and click the Toolbars tab of the displayed dialogue box.

- Click the **New** button to display the screen shown below.

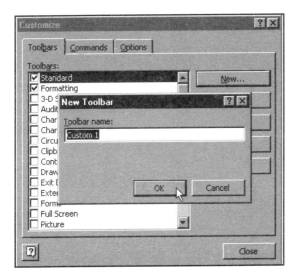

- In the **Toolbar name** text box, type the name you want, and click the **OK** button.

- Finally, click the **Close** button. The new toolbar remains showing on the screen.

You can now use the skills acquired earlier to move and/or copy buttons to the new toolbar. If the newly created toolbar is for 'storing' deleted custom-made buttons, then you might like to hide it by right-clicking it and clearing the check box next to its name in the shortcut menu.

To delete a New Toolbar, select it in the Toolbars list of the Customize dialogue box and press the **Delete** button.

Manipulating Menu Commands

Menu commands can be added to or removed from menus in the same way as buttons can be added to or removed from toolbars. You could even add menus to a button on a toolbar.

For example, to add a command or other item to a menu, do the following:

- Use the **Tools**, **Customize** command to open the Customize dialogue box, then click the Commands tab.

- In the **Categories** box, click a category for the command.

- Drag the command you want from the **Commands** box over the menu. When the menu displays a list of menu options, point to the location where you want the command to appear on the menu, and then release the mouse, as shown below.

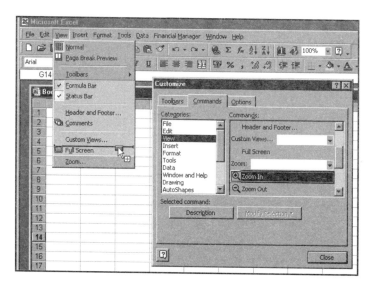

If you don't see the command you want under a particular category, click All Commands in the Categories box.

To remove a command from a list of menu options, do the following:

• Open the Customize dialogue box (you might have to move it out of the way of the drop-down menu options from which you want to remove a command).

• Select the menu option you want to remove and drag it to the editing area of your document, as shown below.

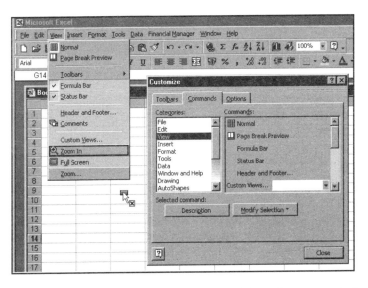

• Release the mouse button to delete the unwanted menu option.

As you can see, manipulating menu options is very similar to manipulating buttons on toolbars, so we leave it to you to explore all the available possibilities - have fun!

Restoring Default Toolbars or Menus

To restore the default buttons on toolbars or menu options, use the **Tools**, **Customize** command to open the Customize dialogue box. Leave the Customize box open (you might need to move it out of the way), and do one of the following:

For a toolbar:

- In the Customize dialogue box, click the Toolbars tab.

- In the **Toolbars** box, click the name of the toolbar you want to reset original buttons and menus on.

- Click the **Reset** button.

For a menu:

- In the Customize dialogue box, click the Commands tab.

- Click the menu that contains the command you want to restore. Right-click the menu command, and then click **Reset** on the shortcut menu.

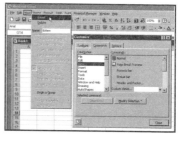

Getting Help on Menus and Toolbars

Excel 2000 has a wealth of help screens on menus and toolbars. To look at some of these, simply activate the Office Assistant, and search for 'menus'. The Assistant returns the list of topics shown to the right. For more topics, click the **See more** button.

If you do not like using the Assistant (we find it intrusive), then deactivate it by clicking the **Options** button, and unchecking the **Use the Office Assistant** box.

Next, use the **Help, Microsoft Excel Help** command, or press **F1**, and click the Answer Wizard tab of the displayed dialogue box. In the **What would you like to do?** box, type 'menus' and press the **Search** button. Left-clicking the first entry under **Select topic to display**, opens the following Microsoft Excel Help screen.

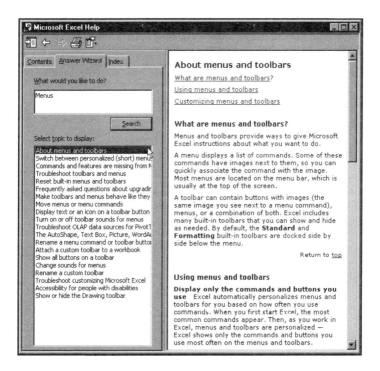

We suggest you spend some time looking at the various help topics in the above help list. You will learn a lot.

Excel Macro Basics

A macro is simply a set of instructions made up of a sequence of keystrokes, mouse selections, or commands stored in a macro file. After saving, or writing, a macro and attaching a quick key combination to it, you can run the same sequence of commands whenever you want. This can save a lot of time and, especially with repetitive operations, can save mistakes creeping into your work.

In Excel there are two basic ways of creating macros. The first one involves the use of Microsoft Visual Basic, the programming language that is common to all Office 2000 applications. With this method, you can write quite complex macro programs directly into a macro file using the Visual Basic editor which allows you, amongst other facilities, to edit, copy, or rename macros. Understanding Visual Basic also makes it easier to program with other Microsoft applications that use the language.

For simple work however, you don't really have to learn to program in Visual Basic, as Excel includes a Macro Recorder which provides you with the second method of generating macros. The Macro Recorder stores the actions you take, including mouse clicks, and the commands you use while working with Excel, which can then be played back (run) to repeat the recorded actions and commands.

Before you record or write a macro, plan the steps and commands you want the macro to perform. This is essential, because if you make a mistake when you record the macro, corrections you make will also be recorded. Each time you record a macro, the macro is stored in a new module attached to a workbook.

Using the Macro Recorder

We will now use the worksheet saved under **Project 3** (see page 58) to show how we can use Excel's Macro Recorder to create a macro to perform 'what-if' type of projections by, say, increasing the 'Wages' bill by 15%.

If you haven't saved **Project 3** on disc, it will be necessary for you to enter the information shown below into Excel so that you can benefit from what is to be introduced at this point. If you have saved **Project 3**, then use the **File, Open** command to display the worksheet shown below.

	A	B	C	D	E	F
	Project 3.xls					
1	*Project Analysis: Adept Consultants Ltd.*					
2						
3		Jan	Feb	Mar	1st Quarter	
4	Income	£ 14,000.00	£ 15,000.00	£ 16,000.00	£ 45,000.00	
5	Costs:					
6	Wages	£ 2,000.00	£ 3,000.00	£ 4,000.00	£ 9,000.00	
7	Travel	£ 400.00	£ 500.00	£ 600.00	£ 1,500.00	
8	Rent	£ 300.00	£ 300.00	£ 300.00	£ 900.00	
9	Heat/Light	£ 150.00	£ 200.00	£ 130.00	£ 480.00	
10	Phone/Fax	£ 250.00	£ 300.00	£ 350.00	£ 900.00	
11	Adverts	£ 1,100.00	£ 1,200.00	£ 1,300.00	£ 3,600.00	
12	Total Costs	£ 4,200.00	£ 5,500.00	£ 6,680.00	£ 16,380.00	
13	Profit	£ 9,800.00	£ 9,500.00	£ 9,320.00	£ 28,620.00	
14	Cumulative	£ 9,800.00	£ 19,300.00	£ 28,620.00		
15						

What we would like to do now is to edit the entries under 'Wages' so that this part of the costs can be increased by 15%. One way of doing this would be to multiply the contents of each cell containing the 'wages' value by 1.15.

To do this, we would start by changing the contents of cell B6 into a formula, by pressing the F2 function key to 'Edit' the value in it by adding an equals sign at the beginning of the entry and then typing '*1.15' at the end of it, which has the effect of multiplying the contents of the cell by 1.15, thus increasing its contents by 15%. We would then press the <Enter> key which would cause the cell pointer to drop to B7, press the ↑ arrow key to move back to cell B6, then press the → arrow key to move to cell C6 and repeat the whole procedure.

The exact steps, after highlighting cell B6, are as follows:

Manual Procedure

Press **F2** to 'Edit' cell
Press the <Home> key to move to beginning of entry
Type = to change entry to formula
Press <End> to move to the end of the entry
Type *1.15
Press the <Enter> key
Press ↑ arrow key
Press → arrow key.

Recording an Excel 2000 Macro

Having opened the **Project 3** file, select cell B6 - the first cell we want to operate on. Then, use the **Tools, Macro, Record New Macro** command which displays the Record Macro dialogue box with the default **Macro name** given as Macro1. This can be changed by you to some more meaningful name, if you so wish.

In the Record Macro dialogue box, we specified that the **Shortcut key** should be Ctrl+w (w for wages), as follows:

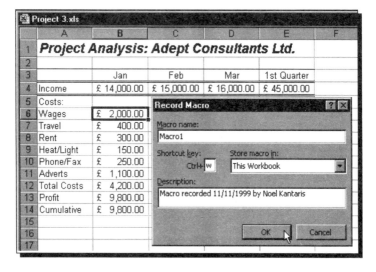

Pressing the **OK** button, causes Excel to display the Stop

Recording button, shown here. Everything you type from now on becomes part of the macro. To start recording our macro, press/type the appropriate key/information, as shown below.

```
F2
<Home>
=
<End>
*1.15
<Enter>
Press ↑ arrow key
Press → arrow key.
```

followed by clicking the Stop Recording button shown above (or by choosing the **Tools, Record Macros, Stop Macros** menu command).

To see the Visual Basic code of your macro, use the **Tools, Macro, Visual Basic Editor** command. If the macro is not in memory a blank Visual Basic screen is displayed in which case you will have to use the **Tools, Macro** command from the Visual Basic menu bar, specify which macro you want to edit by highlighting it, and press the **Edit** button. If the macro is in memory, actioning the editor automatically displays the memory's contents, as shown below.

```
Project 3.xls - Module1 [Code]

(General)                          Macro1

Sub Macro1()

' Macro1 Macro
' Macro recorded 11/11/1999 by Noel Kantaris
'
' Keyboard Shortcut: Ctrl+w
'
    ActiveCell.FormulaR1C1 = "=2000*1.15"
    Range("C6").Select
End Sub
```

Before executing this macro, activate worksheet **Project 3** and change the entry in cell B6 back to its original value of 2000 (it was changed by 15% while you were typing the latest macro commands), then save the macros with the worksheet, but giving your workbook the filename **Autopro 1**. This is a simple precaution because, should things go wrong and your macro does unpredictable things to your worksheet, it will be easier to reopen the original worksheet than it would be to correct it!

To run the first macro, place the cell pointer on cell B6, then press **Ctrl+w**. The shortcut key starts the macro and changes automatically the entry in B6 by 15%.

Visual Basic Programming Advantages

When the macros you write become more complicated, there are many advantages to using Visual Basic rather than using a macro command language that much earlier versions of Excel and other spreadsheet packages used.

In Visual Basic you can assign values directly to variables instead of storing a value in a name as you would have to do in the macro command language. Variables can be made available to all procedures, to just the procedure in a module, or to just a single procedure, thus being far more flexible than names. In addition, in Visual Basic you can define constants to hold static values that you refer to repeatedly.

Reading Visual Basic Code

Referring to our simple example, you can see that Visual Basic has created a macro that is preceded by comment statements (that start with an apostrophe (')) in which you are informed of the name of the macro, who created it and when, and the keyboard shortcut.

The macro commands are placed in between the two keywords **Sub** and **End Sub** which mark the beginning and end of a macro. In general, keywords, variables, operators, and procedure calls are referred to as statements which are the instructions to Excel to perform some action.

The statement

```
ActiveCell.FormulaR1C1 = "=2000*1.15"
```

is the way that Visual Basic enters the formula **=2000*1.15** into the active cell. In Visual Basic terminology; it uses the **Range** object to identify the range you want to change and sets the **Formula** property of the range to assign a formula to the range.

An 'object' is something you control in Visual Basic. Each object has characteristics called 'properties' which control the appearance of the object. Objects also have 'methods' which are actions that they can take.

In Visual Basic, you use:

- Objects (such as Workbooks, Worksheets, Ranges, Charts) to perform a task. Each object has characteristics, called properties, that make that object useful by controlling the appearance or behaviour of an object.

- Properties (such as ActiveCell, ActiveSheet, Value, Selection, ColumnWidth, RowHeight), to examine the condition of an object by returning the value of one of the object's properties (such as a character string for Value, a numeric value for ColumnWidth, True, or False).

- Methods which are actions that objects can do (such as Calculate, Clear, Copy, Justify, or Table). Methods are a part of objects just like properties. The difference between them is that properties have values which are set or returned, while methods are actions you would like an object to perform.

Should you want to learn to program in Visual Basic, then may we suggest you start with the book *Programming in Visual Basic for Windows* (BP346), also published by BERNARD BABANI (publishing) Ltd.

Editing a Macro

A macro can be edited by opening the file that contains it, and using the **Tools, Macro, Visual Basic Editor** command to load the Visual Basic editor, selecting the macro, and pressing the **Edit** button on the displayed dialogue box, as discussed earlier.

Since each of the three months in our worksheet is to be changed, we can edit all Macro1 references to Macro2, copy the highlighted entries and paste them twice before the **End Sub** statement. Next, change these appropriately so that reference is made to the correct amount of wages in the **ActiveCell.Formula** command and the correct cell reference in the **Range().Select** command, as shown below, and save the workbook under the filename **Autopro 2**.

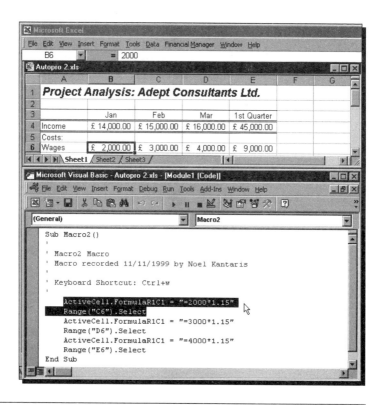

Doing so, also saves Macro2 (which replaces Macro1). If your macro is correct, activating cell B6 and pressing **Ctrl+w** runs it and increases by 15% the values of the wages entries for the three months from those shown on the worksheet window on the previous page.

We could use the same macro to find out the effect of increasing wages by different percentages by editing it, but this would be rather inefficient. A better method is to allocate a cell for the % increase, say cell G5, and edit the macro so that reference to that cell is made in the R1C1 absolute format. In this example, from cell B6 we would have to refer to R[-1]C[5] (Row 1 above present position, Column 5 from present position) which is the reference to cell G5 from B6.

Finally, edit all Macro1 references to Macro2 and save the worksheet under the filename **Autopro 3**. Running the macro now, changes the worksheet entries to those shown below.

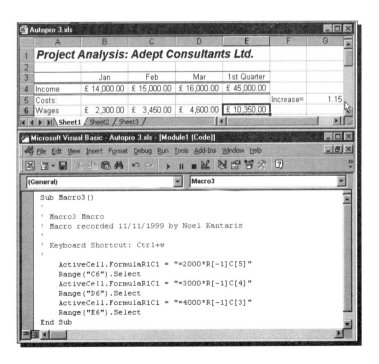

Macro Interaction with Keyboard

A further addition to the above macros could be made to allow for user entry of the 'increment' value from the keyboard, rather than having to edit cell G5. This can be achieved by using the **InputBox()** macro command, which creates a dialogue box, as shown below, and returns the information entered into it.

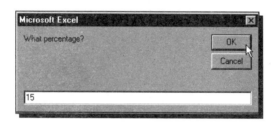

The general format of this macro command is:

```
Variable = InputBox("message")
```

and returns the value typed on the keyboard into the *variable*.

In the macro shown on the next page, we have tried to show the power of Visual Basic without making the example too complicated. First you are asked to give a percentage rate, then the macro calculates the increment and places the value of rate in G5, and stores the original contents of B6:D6 into the three variables, Xjan, Xfeb, and Xmar.

Next, the calculations take place and the results are entered in cell range B6:D6. Finally, a dialogue box is displayed (it can be moved out of the way) asking you to press the **OK** button in order to restore the original contents to the 'Wages' cell range, and changes the contents of G5 to 0 (zero).

Note: This macro only works if the active worksheet is **Sheet1** when you start the macro. If the active sheet is the macro module, then a run time error is encountered.

Finally, save this workbook as **Autopro 4** before attempting to run it.

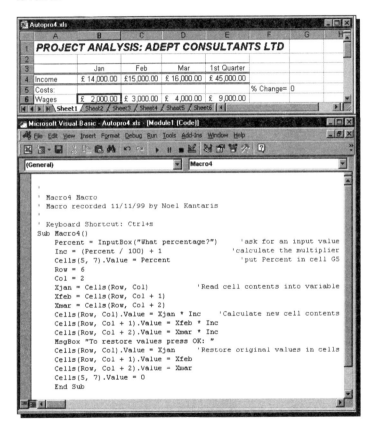

To start the macro, activate cell B6 and press **Ctrl+s**.

Visual Basic has many more statements, commands and functions which can be used to build and run your application in special ways. What we have tried to do here is to introduce you to the subject and give you some idea of the power of this programming language.

That is about it. We hope you have enjoyed reading this book as much as we have enjoyed writing it. Of course Excel 2000 is capable of a lot more than we have discussed here, but what we have tried to do is to give you enough information so that you can forge ahead and explore by yourself the rest of its capabilities.

What follows next is a chapter of exercises with enough guidance to help you get going on your own, followed by a chapter that lists all the functions available to Excel 2000 with an explanation of their required parameters. Finally, we also include a glossary of terms for reference, and in case you have trouble with any jargon that may have crept in.

11

Exercises Using Excel

The following exercises will help you to get going on your own and might be of interest to you. We give you as much guidance as we think is needed for you to complete them by yourself. Good luck!

Compound Interest

To illustrate the behaviour of interest rates, set up an Excel worksheet, as shown below, to calculate the compound interest of money lent over a certain period of time. Plot the resultant yearly interest against time, on the same graph, for three different values of interest rates.

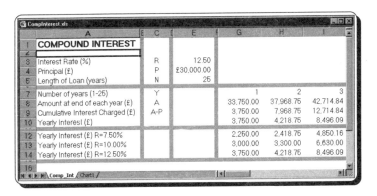

Compound interest is calculated using the formula

$$A = P * (1+R/100)^Y$$

where P is the principal (original money) lent, and A is what it amounts to in time Y years at an interest rate R% per annum. The cumulative interest charged is A-P.

Carry out the calculation on a yearly basis to the full period of the loan (N=25) years, with a constant value of Principal (P=£30,000), but with variable values of interest rate R, namely 7.5, 10 and 12.5%.

Type in your formulae in the worksheet in such a way (by making absolute reference to cells E3 to E5) as to allow you to copy these in the rows below the 'number of years' range that stretches from column G to column AE. You should then only need to change the value of R for the required 'Yearly Interest' to be calculated automatically in row 10.

The **Edit, Fill, Series** command can be used to fill the 'Number of Years' range with incremental data, while the **Edit, Copy** and **Edit, Paste Special, Values** commands can be used to copy the values of 'Yearly Interest' for each value of R to the bottom of the sheet for subsequent graphing. Copying by value is necessary to avoid changes to the data when R is changed.

Format your worksheet as shown on the previous page (or better), and use the information in cells A12:A14 plus G12:EA14, by first highlighting the first cell block, then pressing the <Ctrl> key down and while keeping it depressed, highlighting the second cell block. Next, action the Chart Wizard, select the chart of your choice and specify Sheet2 as the placement area.

Note that you might have to change the font size of the title, axes labels, and legends, and also re-size the chart to get what is shown below.

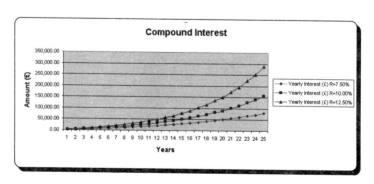

Product Sales Calculations

The first column shown below holds the 'part numbers' which identify a product, while the second and third columns hold the 'cost price' and '% profit' required from the sale of each product. The fourth column holds information on the 'Number of items sold', as follows:

Part No.	Cost Price (£)	% Profit	No. Sold
127	5.6	110	2500
130	6.5	130	1300
133	7	115	2800
136	6.25	125	1900
139	7.25	118	2300
142	7.5	135	2550
145	6.75	120	1800
148	6	133	3200
151	6.55	128	2750
154	7.55	122	1750
157	5.95	119	1950
160	6.16	124	2850

Assuming that the VAT rate is 17.5%, but can be changed subsequently to some other value, use Excel to calculate the following, assuming the relationships given on the next page:

(a) the sale price for each part,
(b) the VAT charged/unit,
(c) the total income,
(c) the sales cost, and
(d) the profit made.

Use the layout shown below for the input data, and the calculated results. You will need to enter the following relationships in columns I to M, respectively:

Column I:

Sale price_unit=Cost price_unit*(I+% profit_unit/100)*(I+VAT%/100)

Column J:

VAT charged_unit=Cost price_unit*(I+% profit_unit/100)*(VAT%/100)

Column K:

Total income=Sale price_unit * No. sold

Column L:

Total sales cost=(Cost price_unit+VAT charged_unit)*No. sold

Column M:

Profit made=(Sale price_unit*No. sold)–Total sales cost.

Format your worksheet as shown below (or better), and make provision for displaying the 'Total Profit made' and 'Total VAT charged' to also be displayed in cells C8 and C9 respectively.

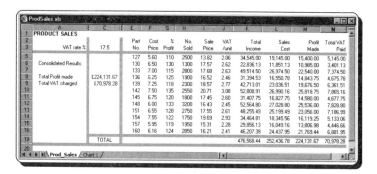

Having done so, then define a graph (see below) to plot Product Part No. versus the profit made for each product and the corresponding volume of sales of each product. Annotate, title and save your graph within the workbook, but on a different sheet from that used for the calculations.

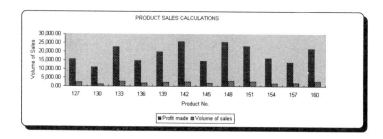

Salary Calculations

A firm employs several persons who are identified by a unique 'works number' only, as shown in the sample table below. The first column of the table holds the 'works number' which identifies a person, while the second column holds the 'annual salary' (in £) of that person. The third and fourth columns of the table hold information relating to the 'overtime' worked (in hours) per month, and the corresponding 'hourly rate' (in £), respectively.

Employee Works No.	Annual Income	Overtime (hrs/month)	Overtime rate (£/hr)
93001	18850	14	14
93002	48500	10	29
93003	69750	6	40
93004	12900	18	16
93005	24350	6	17

The company would like to hold on record, not only the above information for each employee, but also information on the

Monthly Overtime Income,
Total Monthly N.I.,
Monthly Tax on Gross Yearly Income,
Monthly Tax on Overtime,
Total Monthly Income, and
Total Monthly Tax.

We propose to use an Excel worksheet to calculate and hold this information, but for simplicity we will assume that a person pays 11% of their monthly gross salary (excluding overtime) towards N.I. (National Insurance), while what is left is taxed at 25%. In addition, all earnings on overtime are taxed at 40%.

Use the layout suggested below to carry out these calculations. Devise your own formulae for the required calculations. Type in your formulae in the worksheet in such a way (by making absolute reference to cells C2 to C4) as to allow you to copy these easily. You should then only need to change the values of tax rates and/or N.I., for the information in the consolidated area of the worksheet (C9 to C11) to be calculated automatically.

Use the following input values:

Tax Rate X = 25%,
Tax Rate Y = 40%, and
National Insurance = 11%.

Format your worksheet as shown below (or better).

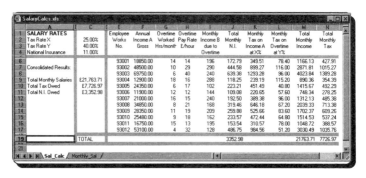

	A	C	E	F	G	H	I	J	K	L	M	N
1	SALARY RATES		Employee Works No.	Annual Income A Gross	Overtime Worked Hrs/month	Overtime Pay Rate £/hour	Monthly Income B due to Overtime	Total Monthly N.I.	Monthly Tax on Income A at X%	Monthly Tax on Overtime at Y%	Total Monthly Income	Total Monthly Tax
2	Tax Rate X	25.00%										
3	Tax Rate Y	40.00%										
4	National Insurance	11.00%										
5			93001	18850.00	14	14	196	172.79	349.51	78.40	1166.13	427.91
6			93002	48500.00	10	29	290	444.58	899.27	116.00	2871.81	1015.27
7	Consolidated Results:		93003	69750.00	6	40	240	639.38	1293.28	96.00	4023.84	1389.28
8			93004	12900.00	18	16	288	118.25	239.19	115.20	890.36	354.39
9	Total Monthly Salaries	£21,763.71	93005	24350.00	6	17	102	223.21	451.49	40.80	1415.67	492.29
10	Total Tax Owed	£7,726.97	93006	11900.00	12	12	144	109.08	220.65	57.60	748.34	278.25
11	Total N.I. Owed	£3,352.98	93007	21000.00	16	15	240	192.50	389.38	96.00	1312.13	485.38
12			93008	34850.00	8	21	168	319.46	646.18	67.20	2039.33	713.38
13			93009	26350.00	11	19	209	259.88	525.66	83.60	1702.37	609.26
14			93010	25480.00	9	18	162	233.57	472.44	64.80	1514.53	537.24
15			93011	16750.00	15	13	195	153.54	310.57	78.00	1048.72	388.57
16			93012	53100.00	4	32	128	486.75	984.56	51.20	3030.49	1035.76
19		TOTAL						3352.98			21763.71	7726.97

Having achieved the above, then define a stacked bar chart (see below), to plot the Total Monthly Income, Total Monthly Tax, and Total Monthly N.I. versus Employee Works No. Annotate, title and save your chart within the workbook, but on a different sheet.

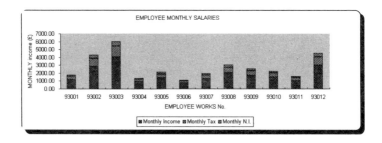

12

Functions

Excel's functions are built-in formulae that perform specialised calculations. Their general format is:

    name(arg1,arg2,...)

where 'name' is the function name, and 'arg1', 'arg2', etc., are the arguments required for the evaluation of the function. Arguments must appear in a parenthesised list as shown above and their exact number depends on the function being used. However, some functions do not require arguments and are used without parentheses. Examples of these are: FALSE, NA, NOW, PI, RAND, TODAY and TRUE.

There are four types of arguments used with functions: numeric values, range values, string values and conditions, the type used being dependent on the type of function. Numeric value arguments can be entered either directly as numbers, as a cell address, a cell range name or as a formula. Range value arguments can be entered either as a range address or a range name, while string value arguments can be entered as an actual value (a string in double quotes), as a cell address, a cell name, or a formula. Condition arguments normally use logical operators or refer to an address containing a logic formula.

Types of Functions

There are several types of functions in Excel 2000, namely, financial, date and time, mathematical and trigonometric, statistical, lookup and reference, database, text, logical, and information. Each type of function requires its own number and type of arguments.

Function arguments, also known as parameters, are listed on the next few pages under the various function categories. To find out in detail how these functions can be used, click the Edit Formula button (▦) to display:

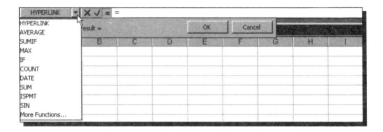

Clicking the down-arrow to the left of the formula bar reveals the most recently used functions. Selecting the last item on the list will display the Paste Function dialogue box which lists all the available functions. Next, choose a function from the displayed list, and activate the Assistant from within this dialogue box. The characteristic yellow banner of the Assistant appears, as shown below, on which you can select to get 'Help with this feature'.

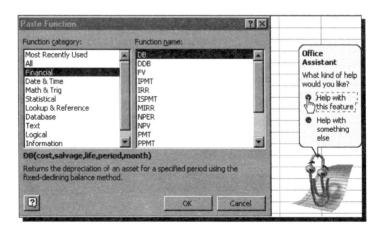

The Assistant then invokes the Excel Help system which displays a whole page of information on each selected function, with examples on how to use it. In what follows, we list all the functions and what they return in a concise form for ease of selection, and so that you can see at a glance what is available.

Financial Functions

Financial functions evaluate loans, annuities, depreciation and cash flows over a period of time, using numeric arguments. Where an optional parameter [Tp] is given the function will calculate for either an ordinary annuity or an annuity due, depending on the value you specified for type Tp. Percentages should be entered either as a decimal (for example, 0.155) or with a percent sign (for example, 15.5%). The various functions and what they return are as follows:

Function	*Returns*
DB(Ct,Sg,Lf,Pd)	The depreciation allowance of an asset with an initial value of Ct, life Lf, a final salvage value Sg for a specified period Pd, using the declining balance method.
DDB(Ct,Sg,Lf,Pd)	The double-declining depreciation allowance of an asset, with original cost Ct, predicted salvage value Sg, life Lf, and period Pd.
FV(Rt,Tm,Pt)	The future value of a series of equal payments, each of equal amount Pt, earning a periodic interest rate Rt, over a number of payment periods in term Tm.

IPMT(Rt,Pr,Tm,Pv)	The interest payment for a given period Pr (which must be between 1 and Tm) of a total term Tm of a loan with present value Pv at a constant interest rate Rt.
IRR(Rg,Gs)	The internal rate of return of range Rg of cash flows, based on the approximate percentage guess Gs.
ISPMT(Rt,Pr,Tm,Pv)	The interest paid during a specific period Pr (which must be between 1 and Tm) of a total term Tm of a loan with present value Pv at an interest rate Rt.
MIRR(Rg,Fr,Rr)	The modified internal rate of return for a series of cashflows in a range Rg, with interest rates Fr, paid on money used in cash flows and Rr received on reinvested cash flows.
NPER(Rt,Pt,Pv,Fv)	The number of periods required for a series of equal payments Pt, with a present-value Pv, to accumulate a future-value Fv, at a periodic interest rate Rt.
NPV(Rt,Rg)	The net present value of the series of future cash flows in range Rg, discounted at a periodic interest rate Rt.
PMT(Rt,Tm,Pv,Fv)	The payment on a loan with present value Pv, at interest rate Rt, for Tm number of payments and future value Fv.

PPMT(Rt,Pr,Tm,Pv,Fv)   The principal portion of the periodic payment on a loan of present value Pv, at interest rate Rt, for payment periods Pr (the number of payment periods in an annuity), leading to a future value Fv.

PV(Rt,Tm,Pt)   The present value of a series of payments, each of amount Pt, discounted at a periodic interest rate Rt, over a number of payment periods in term Tm.

RATE(Tm,Pt,Pv,Fv)   The periodic interest rate necessary for a present value Pv to grow to a future value Fv, over the number of compounding periods in term Tm at Pt payments per period.

SLN(Ct,Sg,Lf)   The straight line depreciation of an asset of cost Ct for one period, given its predicted salvage value Sg, and life Lf.

SYD(Ct,Sg,Lf,Pd)   The sum-of-years' digits depreciation of an asset of cost Ct, given its predicted salvage value Sg, life Lf, and period Pd.

VDB(Ct,Sg,Lf,S,E,*d,s*)   The depreciation of an asset of cost Ct, salvage value Sg, life Lf, over a period from start S to end E. Depreciation-factor *d* and switch *s,* are optional. If *s* is 1 it returns declining balance depreciation for life, else straight-line is used after E.

Date and Time Functions

These generate and use serial numbers with dates having integer serial numbers between 1 and 65380 to represent dates between 1 January, 1900 and 31 December 2078, and time having decimal serial numbers starting with 0.000 at midnight and ending with 0.99999 next midnight. The various functions are:

Function	*Returns*
DATE(Yr,Mh,Dy)	The date number of argument Yr,Mh,Dy.
DATEVALUE(Ts)	The number of days from 1 January 1900 of date string Ts.
DAY(Dn)	The day of the month number (1-31) of date number Dn.
DAYS360(Sn,En)	The number of days between Sn and En, based on a year of 12 months, each of 30 days.
HOUR(Tn)	The hour number (0-23) of time number Tn.
MINUTE(Tn)	The minute number (0-59) of time number Tn.
MONTH(Dn)	The month number (1-12) of date number Dn.
NOW()	The serial number for the current date and time.
SECOND(Tn)	The second number (0-59) of time number Tn.
TIME(Hr,Ms,Ss)	The time number of argument Hr,Ms,Ss.
TIMEVALUE(Ts)	The time number of string Ts.
TODAY()	The current date number.

| WEEKDAY(Dn) | The day of the week from date number Dn in integer form; 0 (Monday) through 6 (Sunday). |
| YEAR(Dn) | Returns the year number (0-199) of date number Dn. |

Mathematical and Trigonometric Functions

These functions evaluate a result using numeric arguments. The various functions and what they return are as follows:

Function	*Returns*
ABS(X)	The absolute value of X.
ACOS(X)	The angle in radians, whose cosine is X (arc cos of X).
ACOSH(N)	The arc (inverse) hyperbolic cosine of number N.
ASIN(X)	The angle in radians, whose sine is X (arc sin of X).
ASINH(N)	The arc (inverse) hyperbolic sine of number N.
ATAN(X)	The angle in radians, between $\pi/2$ and $-\pi/2$, whose tangent is X (arc tan of X - 2 quadrant).
ATAN2(X,Y)	The angle in radians, between π and $-\pi$, whose tangent is Y/X (arc tan of Y/X - 4 quadrant).
ATANH(N)	The arc (inverse) hyperbolic tangent of number N.
CEILING(N,Sig)	The rounded value of N to nearest integer or nearest multiple of significance Sig.

COMBIN(N,Obj)	The number of combinations N for a given number of objects Obj.
COS(X)	The cosine of X (X in radians).
COSH(X)	The hyperbolic cosine of X.
DEGREES(X)	The value in degrees of X radians.
EVEN(X)	The rounded value of X away from 0 to the nearest even integer.
EXP(X)	The value of e raised to the power of X.
FACT(X)	The factorial of X.
FLOOR(N, Sig)	A number N rounded down towards zero by nearest multiple of significance Sig.
INT(X)	The integer part of X.
LN(X)	The natural log (base e) of X.
LOG(X,N)	The log of X to a specified base N.
LOG10(X)	The log (base 10) of X.
MDETERM(Ar)	The matrix determinant of an array.
MINVERSE(Ar)	The matrix inverse of an array.
MMULT(Ar1,Ar2)	The matrix product of two arrays.
MOD(X,Y)	The remainder of X/Y.
ODD(X)	The rounded value of X away from 0 to the nearest odd integer.
PI()	The value of π (3.1415926).

POWER(X,N)	The value of X raised to the power of N.
PRODUCT(Ls)	The result of multiplying the values in list Ls.
RADIANS(X)	The value in radians of X degrees.
RAND()	A random number between 0 and 1.
ROMAN(N,Fm)	The Roman format Fm (as text) of number N.
ROUND(X,N)	The value of X rounded to N places.
ROUNDDOWN(X,N)	The rounded value of X down to the nearest multiple of the power of 10 specified by N.
ROUNDUP(X,N)	The rounded value of X up to the nearest multiple of the power of 10 specified by N.
SIGN(X)	The value of 1 if X is a positive, 0 if X is 0, and −1 if X is negative.
SIN(X)	The sine of angle X (X in rads).
SINH(X)	The hyperbolic sine of angle X (X in rads).
SQRT(X)	The square root of X.
SUBTOTAL(Ls)	The subtotal in a list Ls or a database.
SUM(Rg)	The sum of values in range Rg.
SUMIF(Rg,Cr)	The sum in range Rg that meet a given criteria Cr.
SUMPRODUCT(Ar1,Ar2)	The sum of the products of array components.

SUMSQ(N1,N2)	The sum of the squares of the arguments.
SUMX2MY2(Ar1,Ar2)	The sum of the difference of squares of corresponding values in two arrays.
SUMX2PY2(Ar1,Ar2)	The sum of the sum of squares of corresponding values in two arrays.
SUMXMY2(Ar1,Ar2)	The sum of squares of differences of corresponding values in two arrays.
TAN(X)	The tangent of angle X (X in rads).
TANH(X)	The hyperbolic tangent of angle X (X in rads).
TRUNC(X,N)	The truncated value of X to N decimal places.

Statistical Functions

Statistical functions evaluate lists of values using numeric arguments or cell ranges. The various functions and what they return are as follows:

Function	*Returns*
AVEDEV(Ls)	The average of the absolute deviations of values in list Ls.
AVERAGE(Rg)	The average of values in range Rg.
AVERAGEA(Rg)	The average (arithmetic mean) of values in range Rg, including logical values and text - evaluating text and FALSE as 0, and TRUE as 1.

BETADIST(X,Al,Bt,A,B)	The cumulative beta probability density function.
BETAINV(Pb,Al,Bt,A,B)	The inverse of the cumulative beta probability function.
BINOMDIST(Sc,Tr,Pb,Tp)	The cumulative distribution function if Tp is TRUE, else the probability mass function, with Tr independent trials and Sc successes in trials and Pr probability of success per trial.
CHIDIST(X,Fr)	The chi-square distribution, evaluated at X and Fr degrees of freedom for the sample.
CHINV(X,Fr)	The inverse of the one-tailed probability of the chi-squared distribution.
CHITEST(Rg1,Rg2)	The chi-square test for independence on the data in range Rg1, or a chi-square test for goodness of fit on the data in ranges Rg1 and Rg2.
CONFIDENCE(Al,Sd,Sz)	The confidence interval for a population mean.
CORREL(Rg1,Rg2)	The correlation coefficient of values in ranges Rg1 and Rg2.
COUNT(Ls)	The number of values in a list.
COUNTA(Rg)	The number of non-blank values in a range Rg.
COUNTBLANK(Rg)	The number of blank cells within range Rg.
COUNTIF(Rg, Cr)	The number of non-blank cells within a range Rg.
COVAR(Rg1,Rg2)	The sample covariance of the values in ranges Rg1 and Rg2.

CRITBINOM(Tr,Pb,Al)	The largest integer for which the cumulative binomial distribution is less than or equal to Al, with Tr Bernoulli trials and a probability of success for a single Bernoulli trial Pb.
DEVSQ(Ls)	The sum of squared deviations of the values in list Ls, from their mean.
EXPONDIST(X,Lm,Ds)	The exponential distribution.
FDIST(X,Fr1,Fr2)	The F-distribution at value X with Fr1 and Fr2 degrees of freedom for the first and second samples.
FINV(Pb,Fr1,Fr2)	The inverse of the F probability distribution.
FISHER(X)	The Fisher transformation.
FISHERINV(Y)	The inverse of the Fisher transformation.
FORECAST(X,Yo,Xo)	The value along a linear trend.
FREQUENCY(Rg,Bin)	The frequency distribution as a vertical array Bin.
FTEST(Rg1,Rg2)	The associated probability of an F-test on data in ranges Rg1 and Rg2. Used to determine if two samples have different variances.
GAMMADIST(X,Al,Bt,Cm)	The gamma distribution.
GAMMAINV(Pb,Al,Bt)	The inverse of the gamma cumulative distribution.
GAMMALN(X)	The natural logarithm of the gamma function.
GEOMEAN(Ls)	Returns the geometric mean of the values in list Ls.

GROWTH(Yo,Xo,Xn,Ct)	The values along an exponential trend.
HARMEAN(Ls)	The harmonic mean of the values in list Ls.
HYPGEOMDIST(Ns,Ssiz,Pp,Psiz)	The hypergeometric distribution probability of a given number of successes Ns, given the sample size Ssiz, population success Pp and population size Psiz.
INTERCEPT(Yo,Xo)	The intercept of the linear regression line.
KURT(Rg)	The kurtosis of the values in range Rg.
LARGE(Arr,K)	The largest value in a data set.
LINEST(Yo,Xo,Ct,St)	The parameters of a linear trend.
LOGEST(Yo,Xo,Ct,St)	The parameters of an exponential trend.
LOGINV(Pb,Mn,Sd)	The inverse of the lognormal distribution with parameters mean Mn and standard deviation Sd.
LOGNORMDIST(X,Mn,Sd)	The cumulative lognormal distribution with parameters mean Mn and standard deviation Sd.
MAX(Rg)	The maximum value in a range.
MAXA(Rg)	The maximum value in a range. Does not ignore logical values or text.
MEDIAN(Ls)	The median value in list Ls.

MIN(Rg)	The minimum value in a range.
MINA(Rg)	The minimum value in a range. Does not ignore logical values or text.
MODE(Ls)	The most common value in a data set.
NEGBINOMDIST(Nf,Ns,Pb)	
	The negative binomial distribution that there will be a number of failures Nf before the number of successes Ns, when the constant probability of success is Pb.
NORMDIST(X,Mn,Sd)	The normal cumulative distribution function for X, with a distribution mean Mn and optional standard deviation Sd.
NORMINV(Pb,Mn,Sd)	The inverse of the normal cumulative distribution.
NORMSDIST(X)	The standard normal cumulative distribution.
NORMSINV(Pb)	The inverse of the standard normal cumulative distribution.
PEARSON(Ar1,Ar2)	The Pearson product moment correlation coefficient.
PERCENTILE(Rg,K)	The Kth sample percentile among the values in range Rg.
PERCENTRANK(Ar,X,Sg)	The percentage rank of a value in a data set.
PERMUT(N,Nc)	The number of ordered sequences (permutations) of Nc chosen objects that can be selected from a total of N objects.

POISSON(X,Mn,Cm)	The Poisson distribution (depending on cumulative factor Cm) of X observed events and Mn expected number of events.
PROB(Rgx,Pb,Ll,Ul)	The probability that values in Rgx range are within lower limit Ll and upper limit Ul of probability Pb.
QUARTILE(Ar,Qrt)	The quartile of a data set.
RANK(It,Rg,Od)	The relative size or position of a value It in a range Rg, relative to other values in the range, ranked in order Od.
RSQ(Yo,Xo)	The square of the Pearson product moment correlation coefficient.
SKEW(Rg)	The skewness of the values in range Rg.
SLOPE(Yo,Xo)	The slope of the linear regression line.
SMALL(Ar,K)	The Kth smallest value in a data set.
STANDARDIZE(X,Mn,Sd)	The normalised value of X from a distribution characterised by mean Mn and standard deviation Sd.
STDEV(Rg)	The population standard deviation of values in range Rg.
STDEVA(Rg)	An estimate of the standard deviation based on a sample, including logical values and text.
STDEVP(Rg)	The standard deviation based on the entire population.

STDEVPA(Rg)	The standard deviation based on the entire population, including logical values and text.
STEYX(Yo,Xo)	The standard error of the predicted y-value for each X in the regression.
TDIST(X,Fr,Tr)	The Student's t-distribution, evaluated at X and Fr degrees of freedom for the sample, with test direction Tr.
TINV(Pb,Fr)	The inverse of the Student's t-distribution.
TREND(Xo,Yo,Xn,Cn	The values along a linear trend.
TRIMMEAN(Ar,Pb)	The mean of the interior of a data set.
TTEST(Rg1,Rg2,Tl,Tp)	The probability associated with a Student's t-test.
VAR(Rg)	The sample variance of values in range Rg.
VARA(Rg)	An estimate of the variance based on a sample, including logical values and text.
VARP(Rg)	The variance of values in range Rg based on entire population.
VARPA(Rg)	The variance of values in range Rg based on entire population, including logical values and text.
WEIBULL(X,Al,Bt,Cm)	The Weibull distribution.
ZTEST(Arr,X,Sg)	Returns the two-tailed P-value of a z-test.

Lookup and Reference Functions

This group of functions return values specified by a range reference or array reference. The various functions available and what they return are as follows:

Function	*Returns*
ADDRESS(Rn,Cn)	The cell address specified by row Rn and column Cn.
AREAS(Rf1,Rf2,..)	The number of areas in the list of references.
CHOOSE(K,V0,..,Vn)	The Kth value in the list V0,..,Vn.
COLUMN(Rf)	The column number of a reference.
COLUMNS(Rg)	The number of columns in the range Rg.
GETPIVOTDATA(Pt,Nm)	Returns data stored in a Pivot-Table report. Pt can be a cell or range of cells in the report, a name for the range that contains the PivotTable report, or a label stored in a cell above the PivotTable report. Nm is a text string enclosed in double quotation marks that describes the cell in the PivotTable report that contains the value you want to retrieve.
HLOOKUP(X,Ar,Rn)	The value of indicated cell by performing a horizontal array look-up by comparing the value X to each cell in the top index row in array Ar, then moves down the column in which a match is found by the specified row number Rn.

HYPERLINK(Loc,Fn)	A shortcut to a document on your hard disc, network server of the Internet at specified location and friendly name.
INDEX(Rg,Rn,Cn)	The value of the cell in range Rg at the intersection of row-offset Rn, and column-offset Cn.
INDIRECT(Rf)	The cell reference specified in reference Rf in A1-style.
LOOKUP(Lv,Vr,Rv)	The relative position of an item in an array that matches a specified value in a specified order.
MATCH(Lv,Ar,Mtc)	The relative position of an element in an array Ar that matches the specified value Mtc of a lookup value Lv.
OFFSET(Rf,Rn,C,Ht,Wh)	A reference of a specified height Ht and width Wh offset from another reference Rf by a specified number of rows Rn and columns Cn.
ROW(Rf)	The row number of a reference.
ROWS(Rg)	The number of rows in a range.
TRANSPOSE(Ar)	The transpose of an array.
VLOOKUP(X,Ar,Cn)	The value of indicated cell by performing a vertical table look-up by comparing the value X to each cell in the first index column, in array Ar, then moves across the row in which a match is found by the specified column number Cn.

Database Functions

Database functions perform calculations on a database. The database, called the input range, consists of records, which include fields and field names, like Fd below. A criterion range must be set up to select the records from the database that each function uses. The various functions and what they return are as follows:

Function	*Returns*
DAVERAGE(Db,Fd,Cr)	The average of the values in the field Fd that meet the criteria Cr in a database Db.
DCOUNT(Db,Fd,Cr)	The number of non-blank cells in the field Fd that meet the criteria Cr in a database Db.
DCOUNTA(Db,Fd,Cr)	Counts nonblank cells from a specified database and criteria.
DGET(Db,Fd,Cr)	The single value in the field Fd that meets the criteria Cr in a database Db.
DMAX(Db,Fd,Cr)	The maximum value in the field Fd that meets the criteria Cr in a database Db.
DMIN(Db,Fd,Cr)	The minimum value in the field Fd that meets the criteria Cr in a database Db.
DPRODUCT(Db,Fd,Cr)	The result of the product of the values in the field Fd that meet the criteria Cr in a database Db.
DSTDEV(Db,Fd,Cr)	The standard deviation based on the values in the field Fd that meet the criteria Cr in a database Db.

DSTDEVP(Db,Fd,Cr)   The standard deviation based on the entire population of the values in the field Fd that meet the criteria Cr in a database Db.

DSUM(Db,Fd,Cr)   The sum of the values in the field Fd that meet the criteria Cr in a database Db.

DVAR(Db,Fd,Cr)   The estimated variance based on the values in the field Fd that meet the criteria Cr in a database Db.

DVARP(Db,Fd,Cr)   The variance based on the entire population of the values in the field Fd that meet the criteria Cr in a database Db.

Text Functions

Text functions operate on strings and produce numeric or string values dependent on the function.

Function	*Returns*
CHAR(X)	The character that corresponds to the code number X.
CLEAN(Sg)	The specified string Sg having removed all non-printable characters from it.
CODE(Sg)	The code number for the first character in string Sg.
CONCATENATE(Sg1,Sg2)	One string made up of several strings.
DOLLAR(N,Dm)	A number in text form, using currency format.

EXACT(Sg1,Sg2)	The value 1 (TRUE) if strings Sg1 and Sg2 are exactly alike, otherwise 0 (FALSE).
FIND(Ss,Sg,Sn)	The position at which the first occurrence of search string Ss begins in string Sg, starting the search from search number Sn.
FIXED(N,Dm,Nc)	A number N formatted as text with a fixed number of decimals Dm. Nc is a logical value and if TRUE prevents the inclusion of commas.
LEFT(Sg,N)	The first (leftmost) N characters in string Sg.
LEN(Sg)	The number of characters in string Sg.
LOWER(Sg)	A string Sg with all the letters converted to lowercase.
MID(Sg,Sn,N)	The N characters from string Sg beginning with the character at Sn.
PROPER(Sg)	A string with all words in string Sg changed to first letter in uppercase and the rest in lowercase.
REPLACE(O,S,N,Ns)	A string with N characters removed from original string O, starting at character S and then inserts new string Ns in the vacated place.
REPT(Sg,N)	A repeated string Sg, N times. Unlike the repeating character (\), the output is not limited by the column width.

RIGHT(Sg,N)	The last (rightmost) N characters in string Sg.
SEARCH(Sg1,O,S)	String Sg1 in original string O, starting at character S.
SUBSTITUTE(Sg,O,Ns,N)	A new string Ns substituted for old string O in a string Sg. N specifies which occurrence of the old text you want to replace.
T(X)	A value X converted into text.
TEXT(X,Fm)	A number X formatted into text.
TRIM(Sg)	A string Sg with no leading, trailing or consecutive spaces.
UPPER(Sg)	All letters in string Sg converted to uppercase.
VALUE(Sg)	The numeric value of string Sg.

Logical Functions

Logical functions produce a value based on the result of a conditional statement, using numeric arguments. The various functions and what they return are as follows:

Function	Returns
AND(N1,N2,N3,..)	The logical value 1 (TRUE) if all its arguments are TRUE.
FALSE()	The logical value 0.
IF(Cr,X,Y)	The value X if Cr is TRUE and Y if Cr is FALSE.
NOT(N)	The reverse logic of its argument N.
OR(N1, N2, ..)	The logical value 1 (TRUE) if any argument is TRUE.
TRUE()	The logical value 1.

Information Functions

Information functions perform a variety of advanced tasks, such as looking up values in a table, returning information about cells, ranges or the Excel environment. The various functions and what they return are as follows:

Function	*Returns*
CELL(At,Rg)	Returns the code representing the attribute At of range Rg.
ERROR.TYPE(X)	The error value.
INFO(At)	Returns system information based on the attribute At.
ISBLANK(X)	The value 1 (TRUE), if X is an empty cell.
ISERR(X)	1 (TRUE), if X is an error value except #N/A.
ISERROR(X)	1 (TRUE), if X is any error.
ISLOGICAL(X)	1 (TRUE), if X is a logical value.
ISNA(X)	1 (TRUE), if X contains #N/A.
ISNONTEXT(X)	1 (TRUE), if X is not text.
ISNUMBER(X)	1 (TRUE), if X contains a numeric value.
ISREF(X)	1(TRUE), if X is a reference.
ISTEXT(X)	1 (TRUE), if X is text.
N(X)	A value converted to a number
NA()	The error value #N/A.
TYPE(X)	A number indicating the data type value of X.

13

Glossary of Terms

Add-in	A mini-program which runs in conjunction with another and enhances its functionality.
Address	A unique number or name that identifies a specific computer or user on a network.
Anonymous FTP	Anonymous FTP allows you to connect to a remote computer and transfer public files back to your local computer without the need to have a user ID and password.
Application	Software (program) designed to carry out certain activity, such as word processing, or data management.
Association	An identification of a filename extension to a program. This lets Windows open the program when its files are selected.
Authoring	The process of creating web documents or software.
AVI	Audio Video Interleaved. A Windows multimedia file format for sound and moving pictures.
BASIC	Beginner's All-purpose Symbolic Instruction Code - a high-level programming language.
Bitmap	A technique for managing the image displayed on a computer screen.

Browse	A button in some Windows dialogue boxes that lets you view a list of files and folders before you make a selection.
Browser	A program, like the Internet Explorer, that lets you view Web pages.
Button	A graphic element in a dialogue box or toolbar that performs a specified function.
Cache	An area of memory, or disc space, reserved for data, which speeds up downloading.
Chart	A graphical view of data that is used to visually display trends, patterns, and comparisons.
Client	A computer that has access to services over a computer network. The computer providing the services is a server.
Client application	A Windows application that can accept linked, or embedded, objects.
Clipboard	A temporary storage area of memory, where text and graphics are stored with the Windows cut and copy actions.
Command	An instruction given to a computer to carry out a particular action.
Configuration	A general term referring to the way you have your computer set up.
CPU	The Central Processing Unit; the main chip that executes all instructions entered into a computer.
Database	A collection of data related to a particular topic or purpose.

Dial-up Connection   A popular form of Net connection for the home user, over standard telephone lines.

Direct Connection   A permanent connection between your computer system and the Internet.

Default   The command, device or option automatically chosen.

Desktop   The Windows screen working background, on which you place icons, folders, etc.

Device name   A logical name used by DOS and Windows to identify a device, such as LPT1 or COM1 for the parallel or serial printer.

Dialogue box   A window displayed on the screen to allow the user to enter information.

Directory   An area on disc where information relating to a group of files is kept. Also known as a folder.

Disconnect   To detach a drive, port or computer from a shared device, or to break an Internet connection.

Document   A file produced by an application program.

Domain   A group of devices, servers and computers on a network.

Domain Name   The name of an Internet site, for example www.kantaris.com, which allows you to reference Internet sites without knowing their true numerical address.

Download   To transfer to your computer a file, or data, from another computer.

Drag	To move an object on the screen by pressing and holding down the left mouse button while moving the mouse.
Drive name	The letter followed by a colon which identifies a floppy or hard disc drive.
Embedded object	Information in a document that is 'copied' from its source application. Selecting the object opens the creating application from within the document.
File extension	The suffix following the period in a filename. Windows uses this to identify the source application program. For example .xls indicates an Excel file.
Filename	The name given to a file. In Windows 95/98 and above this can be up to 256 characters long.
Filter	A set of criteria that is applied to data to show a subset of the data.
Folder	An area used to store a group of files, usually with a common link.
Font	A graphic design representing a set of characters, numbers and symbols.
FTP	File Transfer Protocol. The procedure for connecting to a remote computer and transferring files.
Function key	One of the series of 10 or 12 keys marked with the letter F and a numeral, used for specific operations.
GIF	Graphics Interchange Format, a common standard for images on the Web.

Graphic	A picture or illustration, also called an image. Formats include GIF, JPEG, BMP, PCX, and TIFF.
Graphics card	A device that controls the display on the monitor and other allied functions.
GUI	A Graphic User Interface, such as Windows 98, the software front-end that provides an attractive and easy to use interface.
Hard copy	Output on paper.
Hard disc	A device built into the computer for holding programs and data.
Hardware	The equipment that makes up a computer system, excluding the programs or software.
Help	A Windows system that gives you instructions and additional information on using a program.
Home page	The document displayed when you first open your Web browser, or the first document you come to at a Web site.
Host	Computer connected directly to the Internet that provides services to other local and/or remote computers.
HTML	HyperText Markup Language, the format used in documents on the Web.
HTML editor	Authoring tool which assists with the creation of HTML pages.
HTTP	HyperText Transport Protocol, the system used to link and transfer hypertext documents on the Web.

Hyperlink	A segment of text, or an image, that refers to another document on the Web, an Intranet or your PC.
Hypermedia	Hypertext extended to include linked multimedia.
Hypertext	A system that allows documents to be cross-linked so that the reader can explore related links, or documents, by clicking on a highlighted symbol.
Icon	A small graphic image that represents a function or object. Clicking on an icon produces an action.
Image	See graphic.
Interface	A device that allows you to connect a computer to its peripherals.
Internet	The global system of computer networks.
Intranet	A private network inside an organisation using the same kind of software as the Internet.
IP	Internet Protocol - The rules that provide basic Internet functions.
IP Address	Internet Protocol Address - every computer on the Internet has a unique identifying number.
ISP	Internet Service Provider - A company that offers access to the Internet.
JPEG/JPG	Joint Photographic Experts Group, a popular cross-platform format for image files. JPEG is best suited for true colour original images.
Kilobyte	(KB); 1024 bytes of information or storage space.

LAN	Local Area Network - High-speed, privately-owned network covering a limited geographical area, such as an office or a building.
Links	The hypertext connections between Web pages.
Local	A resource that is located on your computer, not linked to it over a network.
Location	An Internet address.
Log on	To gain access to a network.
Megabyte	(MB); 1024 kilobytes of information or storage space.
Megahertz	(MHz); Speed of processor in millions of cycles per second.
Memory	Part of computer consisting of storage elements organised into addressable locations that can hold data and instructions.
Menu	A list of available options in an application.
Menu bar	The horizontal bar that lists the names of menus.
MIDI	Musical Instrument Digital Interface - enables devices to transmit and receive sound and music messages.
MIPS	Million Instructions Per Second; measures speed of a system.
Modem	Short for Modulator-demodulator devices. An electronic device that lets PCs communicate electronically.
Monitor	The display device connected to your PC, also called a screen.

Mouse	A device used to manipulate a pointer around your display and activate processes by pressing buttons.
MPEG	Motion Picture Experts Group - a video file format offering excellent quality in a relatively small file.
Multimedia	The use of photographs, music and sound and movie images in a presentation.
Network	Two or more computers connected together to share resources.
Network server	Central computer which stores files for several linked computers.
OLE	Object Linking and Embedding - A technology for transferring and sharing information among software applications.
Online	Having access to the Internet.
On-line Service	Services such as America On-line and CompuServe that provide content to subscribers and usually connections to the Internet.
Operating system	Software that runs a computer.
Page	An HTML document, or Web site.
Password	A unique character string used to gain access to a network or program.
PATH	The location of a file in the directory tree.
Peripheral	Any device attached to a PC.
Pixel	A picture element on screen; the smallest element that can be independently assigned colour and intensity.

Plug-and-play	Hardware which can be plugged into a PC and be used immediately without configuration.
POP	Post Office Protocol - a method of storing and returning e-mail.
Port	The place where information goes into or out of a computer, e.g. a modem might be connected to the serial port.
PPP	Point-to-Point Protocol - One of two methods (see SLIP) for using special software to establish a temporary direct connection to the Internet over regular phone lines.
Print queue	A list of print jobs waiting to be sent to a printer.
Program	A set of instructions which cause a computer to perform tasks.
Protocol	A set of rules or standards that define how computers communicate with each other.
Query	The set of keywords and operators sent by a user to a search engine, or a database search request.
RAM	Random Access Memory. The computer's volatile memory. Data held in it is lost when power is switched off.
Resource	A directory, or printer, that can be shared over a network.
ROM	Read Only Memory. A PC's non-volatile memory. Data is written into this memory at manufacture and is not affected by power loss.

Scroll bar	A bar that appears at the right side or bottom edge of a window.
Search engine	A program that helps users find information across the Internet.
Serial interface	An interface that transfers data as individual bits.
Server	A computer system that manages and delivers information for client computers.
Shared resource	Any device, program or file that is available to network users.
Site	A place on the Internet. Every Web page has a location where it resides which is called its site.
Software	The programs and instructions that control your PC.
Spooler	Software which handles transfer of information to a store to be used by a peripheral device.
Surfing	The process of looking around the Internet.
SVGA	Super Video Graphics Array; it has all the VGA modes but with 256, or more, colours.
TCP/IP	Transmission Control Protocol/Internet Protocol, combined protocols that perform the transfer of data between two computers. TCP monitors and ensures the correct transfer of data. IP receives the data, breaks it up into packets, and sends it to a network within the Internet.
Text file	An unformatted file of text characters saved in ASCII format.

TIFF	Tagged-Image File Format - a popular graphic image file format.
Tool	Software program used to support Web site creation and management.
Toolbar	A bar containing icons giving quick access to commands.
Toggle	To turn an action on and off with the same switch.
TrueType fonts	Fonts that can be scaled to any size and print as they show on the screen.
UNIX	Multitasking, multi-user computer operating system that is run by many computers that are connected to the Internet.
Upload/Download	The process of transferring files between computers. Files are uploaded from your computer to another and downloaded from another computer to your own.
URL	Uniform Resource Locator, the addressing system used on the Web, containing information about the method of access, the server to be accessed and the path of the file to be accessed.
User ID	The unique identifier, usually used in conjunction with a password, which identifies you on a computer.
Virtual Reality	Simulations of real or imaginary worlds, rendered on a flat two-dimensional screen but appearing three-dimensional.
Virus	A malicious program, downloaded from a web site or disc, designed to

	wipe out information on your computer.
WAIS	Wide Area Information Server, a Net-wide system for looking up specific information in Internet databases.
WAV	Waveform Audio (.wav) - a common audio file format for DOS/Windows computers.
Web	A network of hypertext-based multimedia information servers. Browsers are used to view any information on the Web.
Web Page	An HTML document that is accessible on the Web.
WINSOCK	A Microsoft Windows file that provides the interface to TCP/IP services.
Wizard	A Microsoft tool that asks you questions and then creates an object depending on your answers.

Index

Companion Discs

COMPANION DISCS are available for most computer books written by the same author(s) and published by BERNARD BABANI (publishing) LTD, as listed at the front of this book (except for those marked with an asterisk). These books contain many pages of file/program listings. There is no reason why you should spend hours typing them into your computer, unless you wish to do so, or need the practice.

ORDERING INSTRUCTIONS

To obtain companion discs, fill in the order form below, or a copy of it, enclose a cheque (payable to **P.R.M. Oliver**) or a postal order, and send it to the address given below. **Make sure you fill in your name and address** and specify the book number and title in your order.

Book No.	Book Name	Unit Price	Total Price
BP		£3.50	
BP		£3.50	
BP		£3.50	
Name .... Address	Sub-total	£............	
	P & P (@ 45p/disc)	£............	
	Total Due	£............	

Send to: P.R.M. Oliver, CSM, Pool, Redruth, Cornwall, TR15 3SE

PLEASE NOTE

The author(s) are fully responsible for providing this Companion Disc service. The publishers of this book accept no responsibility for the supply, quality, or magnetic contents of the disc, or in respect of any damage, or injury that might be suffered or caused by its use.

Notes